Design School
type

Brimming with creative inspiration, how-to projects, and useful information to enrich your everyday life, Quarto Knows is a favorite destination for those pursing their interests and passions. Visit our site and dig deeper with our books into your area of interest: Quarto Creates, Quarto Cooks, Quarto Homes, Quarto Lives, Quarto Drives, Quarto Explores, Quarto Gifts, or Quarto Kids.

© 2017 Quarto Publishing Group USA, Inc.

First Published in 2017 by Rockport Publishers, an imprint of
The Quarto Group,
100 Cummings Center, Suite 265-D,
Beverly, MA 01915, USA.
T (978) 282-9590
F (978) 283-2742
QuartoKnows.com

Rockport Publishers titles are also available at discount for retail, wholesale, promotional, and bulk purchase. For details, contact the Special Sales Manager by email at specialsales@quarto.com or by mail at The Quarto Group, Attn: Special Sales Manager, 401 Second Avenue North, Suite 310, Minneapolis, MN 55401, USA.

10 9 8 7 6 5 4 3 2

ISBN: 978-1-63159-320-8

Digital edition published in 2017
eISBN: 978-1-63159-439-7

Library of Congress Cataloging-in-Publication Data available

Design: Poulin + Morris Inc.

Printed in China

Design School

type

**A Practical Guide
for Students and Designers**

Richard Poulin

Table of Contents

Here

TYPE

can serve you

J. M. BUNDSCHO, INC.

Advertising Typography & Design

CHICAGO

Introduction

Typography is the craft of endowing human language with a durable, visible form.

—Robert Bringhurst, *The Elements of Typographic Style*

ype is the descriptive term used for letterforms—alphabet, numbers, and punctuation—that, when used together, create words, sentences, and narrative form. The term typeface refers to the design of all the characters referenced above, unified by common visual elements and characteristics. Typography is designing with type.

Type is a unique element in the graphic designer's vocabulary because it has dual functions. It can function on its purest level as any fundamental visual element such as point, line, form, shape, and texture in a composition. However, its primary function is verbal and visual—it is to be read. When type has a relationship only to its verbal meaning, its communicative character lacks visual impact. When type reflects a visual treatment that enhances both its verbal and visual meaning, it is perceived on multiple levels, not only intellectually but also sensually and, more importantly, emotionally.

Type, of course, is all around us. The goal of any graphic designer is not to just place type on a printed or digital page, but rather to understand it and use it effectively in all areas of graphic design. The selection and choice of type, as well as its size, alignment, style, color, and spacing all are critical considerations for the graphic designer.

Since the beginning of mankind, we have needed to communicate our lives to one another. After we learned to speak verbally, we then spoke visually by leaving crude marks on walls and surfaces. From cave paintings and hieroglyphics to Roman inscriptions and medieval scripts, communicating experiences to one another has been a common human denominator for telling our stories at any given time. As our world has become more complex, so has the means by which we communicate those stories in their many forms and media. The most universal means throughout history has been, and will continue to be, type.

For more than five hundred years, type has been an essential visual communicator that continues to reflect civilization, culture, technology, and the human condition at any given time period. Its evolution follows the parallel developments of human communication needs, print technologies from the rudimentary hand to mechanical printing, to the invention of typesetting such as the Linotype and Monotype systems, to the twentieth-century developments of phototypesetting and digital typesetting methodologies.

Graphic design provides a means for you to express your own imagination in ways that do not rely solely upon spoken or written language. Every element used in graphic design, such as type, has the potential to express something specific. Although the explanation and ultimate use of design elements and principles may seem cut-and-dry, the quality of these elements and principles is perceived solely through the expression of the total message by a graphic designer.

Type is one of the most powerful forms of visual expression and communications. When used in combination with imagery, color, and other relevant design elements, it can convey a memorable and timeless message that will always be associated with a specific human emotion.

Typography in practice is the process of arranging letters, words, and text for almost any context imaginable. It is among the most important design principles you need to master for creating effective and meaningful graphic design. Graphic designers learn the nuances of typography in order to use it creatively, with imagination and a sense of exploration, while maintaining respect for its rules and traditions.

Design School: Type is a back-to-basics, practical guide on the rules and practices of type. The foundation of any successful graphic designer relies upon their understanding of the fundamentals of type, a crucially important skill which underpins almost every other aspect of graphic design. This book provides an in-depth understanding of the basic elements and principles of type—what they are, why they are important, and how to use them effectively.

Design School: Type not only explores the graphic design student experience; it includes work by some of the most successful and renowned design practitioners from around the world and how they have applied these basic principles to their work. By examining both student and professional work, *Design School: Type* is also a more meaningful, memorable, and inspiring guide for students, as well as novice practitioners starting their professional careers.
¶

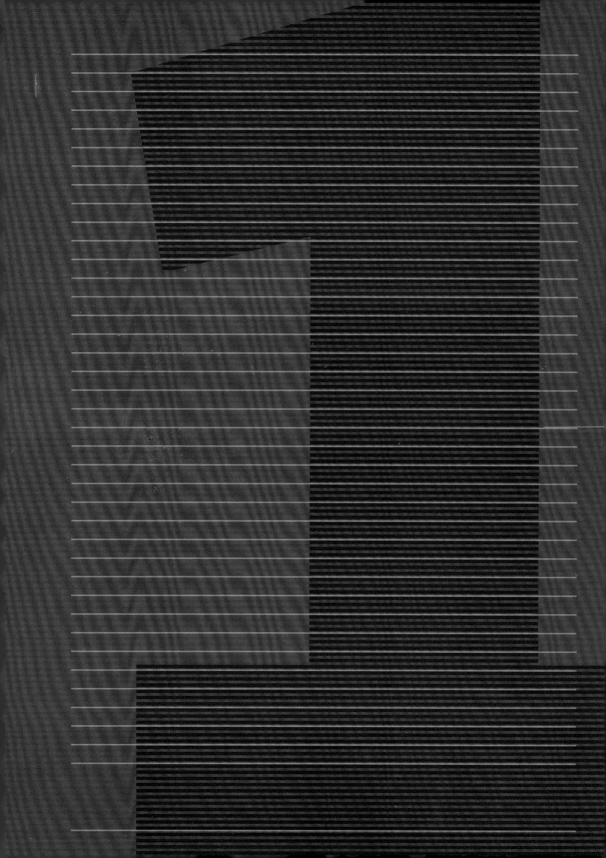

Section 1

Type Classifications

This section examines in detail the history of type through the organization and classification of type styles and time periods. Each type classification is presented with an overview, brief biographies of prominent type designers, visual characteristics, and applications, as well as sidebars covering distinct developments or features of each type classification.

How does a graphic designer determine, among the thousands of typefaces available, which font or fonts might fulfill a specific need? While most typefaces are classified into three categories—serif, sans serif,

Humanist

JENSON (1471)

Old Style

GARAMOND (CA. 1530)

Transitional

BASKERVILLE (1757)

Modern

BODONI (1798)

Slab Serif

CLARENDON (1845)

**Sans Serif
Grotesque**

FRANKLIN GOTHIC (1903)

**Sans Serif
Neo-Grotesque**

HELVETICA (1956)

**Sans Serif
Geometric**

FUTURA (1927)

**Sans Serif
Humanist**

GILL SANS (1927)

Glyphic

ALBERTUS (1940)

Script

KÜENSTLER SCRIPT (1957)

Decorative

SAPHIR (1953)

Blackletter

GOUDY TEXT (1928)

and script—it is a limited and somewhat shortsighted classification system. One method for familiarizing yourself with typefaces and their unique characteristics and attributes, as well as understanding their historical development and potential applications, is to use a more detailed and accurate system of type classification.

All type classification systems use the historical development of type, from the fifteenth century to the present day, as their organizational framework. While there are no two type classification systems that agree upon specific categorization of every typeface, these systems still remain an effective and informative reference guide for identifying and utilizing the number of typefaces available today.

An early type classification system by typographer Francis Thibaudeau (French, 1860–1925) was based on four broad categories of typefaces, namely Antiques (Sans Serifs), Egyptiennes (Slab Serifs), Didots (moderns), and Elzévirs (typefaces with triangular serifs).

A basic system for classifying typefaces was also devised in the nineteenth century, when printers sought to identify a heritage for their own craft analogous to that of art history. Humanist letterforms are closely connected to calligraphy and the movement of the hand. Transitional and modern typefaces are more abstract and less organic. These three main groups correspond roughly to the Renaissance, Baroque, and Enlightenment periods in art and literature. Historians and critics of typography have since proposed more finely detailed schemes that attempt to better capture the diversity

of letterforms. Designers in the twenty-first century have continued to create new typefaces based on these historic characteristics.

The first and most universally used type classification system, Vox-ATypl, was developed in 1954 by typographer Maximilien Vox (French, 1894–1974), adopted in 1962 by the Association Typographique Internationale (ATypl) and in 1967 as the British Standards Classification of Typefaces (BS 2961:1967). Subsequent attempts in creating universal type classification systems were also made by ATypl (1961), DIN (1964), Lawson RIT (1971), Bitstream (1986), Linotype (1988), and Adobe (1991).

The following type classification system is a simplified, practical reference tool for graphic designers and is based on the anatomical characteristics of letterforms, with several sub-categories.

Classification Categories
Humanist
Old Style
Transitional
Modern
Slab Serif
Sans Serif (Grotesque, Neo-Grotesque,
       Geometric, Humanist)
Glyphic
Script (Formal, Casual, Calligraphic)
Decorative
Blackletter (Textura, Bastarda,
       Fraktur, Rotunda)

Examples of each type classification with brief descriptions of their historical development and their primary visual characteristics are provided on the following pages.

Jenson (1471)

Nicolas Jenson (French, 1420–1480)

abcdefghijklmnop

qrstuvwxyz

ABCDEFGHIJK

LNOPQRSTUV

WXYZ

0123456789

Type Designer Profile:
Nicolas Jenson
(French, 1420–1480)

Nicholas Jenson studied punch cutting (see page 21), printing, and typography in Mainz, the German birthplace of typography, before establishing his own printing press in Venice, Italy. He was one of the first printers to use type based on the traditional Roman letter rather than the dark Blackletter (see page 85) or Gothic type found in earlier German printed books. His early Roman letterforms have strong vertical stems and reflect the transition from thick to thin strokes originally created by a broad-nibbed pen.

Born in northeastern France in 1420, Jenson initially apprenticed at the Paris Mint before being promoted to Master of the Mint in Tours. In 1458, Charles VII sent him to Mainz to learn more about the newly invented printing press. His Roman typeface, first used in 1470 in Eusebius's *De Praeparatio Evangelica*, was designed specifically to typographic ideals and in rejection of prevalent manuscript models. Jenson emigrated to Venice in 1470 and was an influential figure in making Venice one of the premier centers of the printing press during the Renaissance era.

His Roman typeface greatly influenced printing and typography five hundred years later during its revival in the late-nineteenth and twentieth centuries and included typefaces such as Golden (William Morris, 1890), Cloister Old Style (Morris Fuller Benton, ca. 1897), Kennerley (Frederic Goudy, 1911), Centaur (Bruce Rogers, 1914, see page 19), and Adobe Jenson (Robert Slimbach, 1995).

Humanist

Humanist typefaces designed in the late fifteenth century mark the start of the refinement of typographic form from centuries of handwritten and calligraphic-based letterforms to a more articulated and delineated type genre.

While this classification represents a short span of type history of approximately twenty-five years, it includes the first Roman typefaces developed in the fifteenth century by Venetian engravers, printers, and type designers such as Nicolas Jenson (1420–1480).

Visual Characteristics:

Humanist

Debx O

Stroke
Low to moderate
contrast between thick
and thin strokes.

Letterform
Small x-height; distinct
angled cross bar of
the lowercase e; circular
bowls; high ascenders
and deep descenders

Axis (or Stress)
Strong inclined stress
reflecting earlier
letterforms drawn with
a broad-nibbed pen.

Visual Characteristics

The design of Humanist typefaces was influenced by the Carolingian minuscule (see page 21), which was imposed by Charlemagne during his reign as emperor of the Holy Roman Empire. Since the late fifteenth century, Humanist typefaces (also known at the time as old face Venetians) represented the first major stylistic development in type design, as well as the introduction of typographic letterforms that were developed for printing, as opposed to handwritten letterforms for manuscripts.

Rather than referencing the formal Textura or Fraktur Blackletter typefaces (see page 85) that were used extensively in illuminated manuscripts and Gutenberg's bible (ca. 1455), Humanist typefaces were developed to mirror the hand-drawn Latin letterforms of intellectuals and scribes of the time. These typefaces are extremely calligraphic in appearance and possess a strong inclined stress reflecting earlier letterforms drawn with a broad-nibbed pen. This angled characteristic is evident in the bowls of their lowercase characters, as well as the distinct angled cross bar of the lowercase "e." Other distinctive visual characteristics include minimal contrast between thick and thin strokes, rounded forms with short and thick bracketed serifs, ascenders with slanted serifs, and a small x-height.

Applications

While Humanist typefaces have considerable visual character, they are limited in their practical applications.

Due to their strong calligraphic influence that is clearly evident in their strong axis,

Revival Humanist Typeface:

Centaur (1914)

Bruce Rogers (American, 1870–1957)

abcdefghijklmnop

qrstuvwxyz

ABCDEFGHIJKL

MNOPQRSTU

VWXYZ

0123456789

Type Designer Profile:

Bruce Rogers

(American, 1870-1957)

Born in Indiana in 1870, Bruce Rogers was an American graphic and type designer considered by some the greatest book designer of the twentieth century. He was known for a classical approach to typography and page layout and for dismissing twentieth-century modernism.

After completing his studies at Purdue University, Rogers worked as an artist for the *Indianapolis News*. During this period, he became interested in publishing and producing fine books, so he moved to Boston, where he became a freelance graphic designer for publisher Louis Prang & Co. It was here that he designed his first typeface, Montaigne (1901), a Venetian-style design named for the earliest book in which it appeared, a 1903 limited edition of *The Essays of Montaigne*.

In 1912, Rogers moved to New York City where he worked both as a freelance graphic designer and as house book designer for The Metropolitan Museum of Art. During his tenure at the Museum, he designed his most famous typeface, Centaur (see page 19; right), for the 1915 limited edition of Maurice de Guérin's *The Centaur*. This typeface, with its fluid, calligraphic-like strokes, is a revival of Jenson (1471, see page 16) by Nicolas Jenson (French, 1420–1480; see page 17).

In subsequent years, Rogers worked extensively as a typographic advisor and book designer for Mount Vernon Press, Harvard University Press, Monotype Corporation, and Oxford University Press.

THE BANQUET OF PLATO

APOLLODORUS. I think that the subject of your inquiries is still fresh in my memory; for yesterday, as I chanced to be returning home from Phaleros, one of my acquaintance, seeing me before him, called out to me from a distance, jokingly, 'Apollodorus, you Phalerian, will you not wait a minute?'—I waited for him, and as soon as he overtook me, 'I have just been looking for you, Apollodorus,' he said, 'for I wish to hear what those discussions were on Love, which took place at the party, when Agathon, Socrates, Alcibiades, and some others met at supper. Some one who heard it from Phœnix, the son of Philip, told me that you could give a full account, but he could relate nothing distinctly him-

angular cross bars, and characterized by deep descenders, high ascenders, and low x-heights, they require minimum leading. Their relatively small body size, irregular profiles, and minimal counters collectively influence their legibility and readability at smaller sizes.

Seminal Humanist Typefaces:
Adobe Jenson (Robert Slimbach, 1995)
Calluna (Jos Buivenga, 2009)
Cloister (Morris Fuller Benton, 1897)
Golden (William Morris, 1890)
Horley Old Style
      (Frank Hinman Pierpont, 1925)
Kennerley (Frederic Goudy, 1911)
Ruit (Gerrit Noordzij, 1980)
¶

Historical Influence:
The Punch Cutter

In traditional typographic terms, the punch cutter was a highly skilled craftsman or technician who transferred the outline profiles of the design of a typeface to one end of a steel bar. These profiles would be cut or "punched" into the steel so that copper matrices could be made for casting type for typesetting in letterpress printing.

Specifically, the punched steel bar or punch (see below left) would be used to create a mold by using the punch on a softer metal, such as copper, to create a matrix. Then, a molten metal alloy of lead, antimony, and tin would be flowed into the mold to produce a single piece of type or matrix (see below right), ready for use in typesetting. The small letterforms located at the base of the matrix are founders' marks.

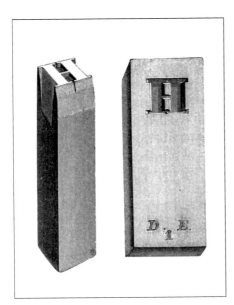

Historical Influence:
The Carolingian Minuscule

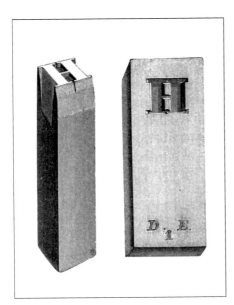

The Carolingian or Caroline minuscule (see above) was the first typographic standard in Europe that made the Latin alphabet recognizable to a majority of literate regions throughout the Holy Roman Empire from approximately 800 to 1200 CE. It was named for the abbot and head of the scriptorium at the Corbie Abbey, Amiens, France in 780 CE.

Codices and Christian texts were written in Carolingian minuscules which created a uniformity of rounded shapes that formed distinct and legible characters that enhanced readability. Capital letters and consistent word spacing also became a standard with Carolingian minuscules.

The minuscule subsequently developed into Blackletter (see page 85) which in later years became somewhat obsolete, though its revival during the fourteenth through sixteenth centuries of the Italian Renaissance formed the basis of more recently designed Scripts.

In the twentieth century, Émigré type designer Zuzana Licko (see page 33) introduced her interpretation of a minuscule to her Modern revivalist typeface Filosofia (1996).

Core Old Style Typeface:
Garamond (ca. 1530)
Claude Garamond (French, 1480–1561)

abcdefghijklmno

pqrstuvwxyz

ABCDEFGHIJK

LMNOPQRSTU

VWXYZ

0123456789

Type Designer Profile:

Claude Garamond

(French, 1480–1561)

Claude Garamond worked with several punch cutters before starting a career of his own in the early 1520s in Paris where he designed many Roman typefaces, including two italics and a full set of chancery Greeks.

In the late 1520s, printer and classical scholar Robert Estienne (French, 1503–1559) commissioned Garamond to design typefaces for several publications, including the 1530 edition of *Paraphrasis* by Erasmus. Following the positive reception and success of his Roman typeface, Garamond was asked by King Francois I of France to design a Greek typeface for his exclusive use, now known as Grecs du Roi (ca. 1549; see right).

By the end of the sixteenth century, Garamond's Roman typeface had become the standard type style used extensively throughout Europe and was still in use two hundred years later.

Old Style

Old Style typefaces, also known as Garaldes, cover approximately a two hundred-year period (late-fifteenth century to mid-eighteenth century) in the development and refinement of typographic form from a calligraphic–based aesthetic to the profiles and forms designed by the punch cutter (see page 21). This type classification includes Bembo (Francesco Griffo, ca. 1450–1518), Garamond (Claude Garamond, ca. 1530), and Goudy (Frederic Goudy, 1915), which are all classified as Old Style typefaces.

The primary model for Old Style was based on typefaces designed by the notable Renaissance publisher and printer Aldus Manutius (Italian, 1450–1515), and cut by the punch cutter Francesco Griffo (Italian, ca. 1450–1518) for the Aldine Press during the late fifteenth century. Cardinal Bembo's *De Aetna*, published by Manutius in 1495, provided the genesis for this new type classification, as well as its name to one of this classification's seminal examples—Bembo. Because of their attractiveness and legibility, these typefaces became the publishing models for the next two hundred and fifty years.

E e k O

Stroke	Letterform	Terminal	Axis (or Stress)
Minimal contrast in stroke weight; hairlines tend to be heavier.	**Horizontal cross bar of the lowercase e.**	**Serifs are bracketed; head serifs are angled.**	**Oblique stress of curved strokes inclines to the left.**

While this type classification was influenced by the first romans or Humanist typefaces created in Venice by printer Nicolas Jenson (see page 17) in the later part of the fifteenth century, their further development was guided by type designers such as Claude Garamond (French, 1480–1561, see page 23), Robert Granjon (French, 1513–1589), and Jean Jannon (French, 1580–1658) in the sixteenth century as they produced new and refined forms of this genre. Finally, mid-eighteenth century Old Style typefaces designed in England by William Caslon (English, 1692–1766) appeared heavier and more visually substantial, representing the full development of this type classification.

Robert Granjon was a French punch cutter and type designer who worked in Paris, Lyon, Antwerp, Frankfurt, and Rome. He designed many Renaissance and Mannerist Romans, italics, Greeks, a Cyrillic, Hebrews, and the first successful Arabic typeface.

His most notable contribution to type design was his italic type, Parnagon de Granjon (ca. 1550), which possessed a greater slant angle, slanted Roman capitals, and a reduced stroke weight. These visual characteristics, as well as an extreme contrast between its thick and thin strokes, gave it a beautiful appearance but sacrificed legibility and readability. Nevertheless, Granjon's italic was the primary influence for italic type design until the revival of the Arrighi model in 1920. (Ludovico Degli Arrighi's (Italian, ca. 1480–1527) italic typeface (ca. 1527) derived from Renaissance Italian handwritten scripts known as *cursiva humanistica*).

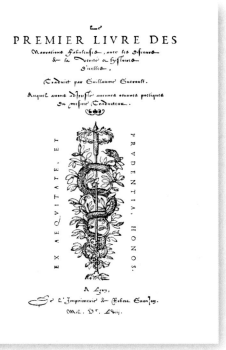

PREMIER LIVRE DES

Le Premier Livre des Narrations Fabuleuses title page, 1558
Robert Granjon (French, 1513–1589)
The title page for *Le Premier Livre des Narrations Fabuleuses* (*The First Book of Fabulous Stories*) shows Granjon's cursiva letterforms, known as **Parnagon de Granjon, which he used for the text of this 127-page publication. The serpent ornament framed by vertical roman capitals is Granjon's trademark.**

French punch cutter, type designer, and printer Jean Jannon studied and trained with Robert Estienne (French, 1503–1559), a printer and classical scholar, in Paris. He developed his first type specimen, Caractères de l'Université, in 1621. Subsequently, Jannon's roman typefaces were used by the Imprimerie Royale and in an edition of Cardinal Richelieu's memoirs in 1642. These typefaces are considered to be the first Baroque typefaces.

William Caslon was well known in eighteenth-century England for designing typefaces that possessed crisp, upright characters. He was the first British type designer of any renown, responsible for ending British printers' dependence on using imported Dutch and French typefaces that had dominated printing and publishing throughout the seventeenth century.

Born in Worcestershire, England, Caslon began his career as an engraver before becoming interested in punch cutting and type design in 1722. His first Roman typeface, the Pica Roman (ca. 1725) was closely based on a Dutch typeface. His subsequent typefaces included Caslon English, Small Pica No. 1, Long Primer No. 2, and the celebrated Great Primer Roman. He was one of the first type designers to publish a specimen sheet (see page 164) illustrating almost the full range of his Roman typefaces to date.

Caslon's typefaces marked the end of the Old Style era, and the appearance of some of the visual characteristics evident in later Transitional style letterforms. William Caslon was undeniably the most important member of the Caslon family due to his contributions to type design which became the standard for roman typography throughout Great Britain for the next 200 years. The Caslon family continued in the type foundry business until 1938 as the Stephenson Blake & Co. Foundry.

Visual Characteristics
Old Style typefaces include some of the most beautiful, legible, and well-designed text typefaces in use today. They are primarily based on roman proportions, therefore do not have strong contrasts in stroke weights.

Revival Old Style Typeface:
Sabon (1964)
Jan Tschichold (German, 1902–1974)

abcdefghijklmno

pqrstuvwxyz

ABCDEFGHIJKL

MNOPQRSTU

VWXYZ

0123456789

Type Designer Profile:

Jan Tschichold

(German, 1902–1974)

Jan Tschichold was one of the most controversial and influential graphic designers and typographers of the twentieth century. He was born in Leipzig, Germany in 1902. As a teenager, he studied calligraphy, typography, and engraving, and continued his formal studies at the Academy for Graphic Arts and Book Trades in Leipzig and at the School of Arts & Crafts in Dresden.

Following a visit to the Weimar Bauhaus exhibition in 1923, he immediately became an advocate of the "new typography," which celebrated abstract modernist principles such as asymmetrical layouts and Sans Serif typefaces. Years later, he became as well known for denouncing these ideals and returning to traditional design principles. He represented these ideals and principles in his extensive work for Penguin Books as shown here in his book cover (see right) for *William Shakespeare: The Tragedy of King Lear* (1949) with an engraved Shakespeare portrait by Reynolds Stone (1909–1979).

Tschichold began his teaching career at the Leipzig Academy, and from 1926 to 1933 he taught at the German School for Master Printers in Munich. He designed several typefaces during the 1920s and 1930s in Germany; however most of them were lost during World War II. He designed his well-known typeface, Sabon (based on the sixteenth century typefaces of Claude Garamond), in 1964 which remains widely used today.

In 1958, the American Institute of Graphic Arts in New York presented him with its highest honor, the AIGA Medal, and in 1965, the Royal Society of Arts in London made him the first Honorary Royal Designer for Industry.

Image: Penguin Books Ltd. ©1970.

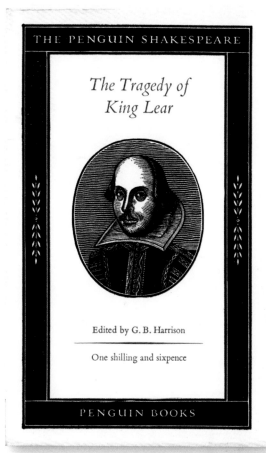

The stress of their curved strokes is noticeably oblique, a smaller x-height defines their lowercase letters, terminals are pear-shaped, and lowercase counters are small.

Earlier Venetian-based typefaces (and their revivals) within this type classification have ascenders that are approximately the same height as their capitals with subsequent developments exhibiting more pronounced

The First Italic Typeface

EMPEREGO

tantuminunquám

s   V *exatus toties rat*

Codri ?

I *mpune ergo mihi*

togatus?

H *ic elegos?impune diem consumpseri*

T *elephus? aut summi plena iam mar*

S *criptus, et in tergo nec dum finitus, O*

N *ota magis nulli domus est sua, quam*

While it is now assumed that every roman typeface is accompanied by its italic equivalent, early Humanist and Old Style typefaces were not initially designed with italic versions.

The first italic typeface was designed during this time period and was originally conceived as a stand-alone text typeface, not as an accompanying version to a roman font. In 1501, these typefaces were primarily developed for use in small-format books where page sizes demanded more condensed and close-set characters which allowed for more words on each line.

Aldus Manutius (Italian, 1450–1515) and Francesco Griffo (Italian, ca. 1450–1518) are credited for the invention of italic type (see above), which made its first appearance in a 1501 edition of *Virgil*, based on a script used by the Papal Chancery. Griffo designed two other italics: one for the printer Geronimo Soncino (d. 1533) for his book *Petrarch of 1503*, and one for himself. Griffo used the latter when, after Manutius's death, he published small editions on his own in his native Bologna. Though the pair had a successful idea, later designers followed other models for their italics.

or taller ascenders with angled head serifs. Additionally, diagonal cross bars on the lowercase "e" are apparent, whereas later Old Style typefaces possess horizontal cross bars.

Other unique visual characteristics include hairline strokes that appear heavier than conventional hairlines, bracketed serifs, and a strong inclined stress.

Applications

Like their Humanist predecessors, Old Style typefaces possess distinctive visual characteristics yet have limited applications.

Due to the strong calligraphic influence that is clearly evident in their strong axis, angular cross bars, and characterized by deep descenders, high ascenders, and low x-heights, they require minimum leading. Their relatively small body size, irregular profiles, and minimal counters collectively influence their legibility and readability at smaller sizes.

Seminal Old Style Typefaces:

Bembo (Francesco Griffo, 1495)

Berkeley (Frederic Goudy, 1938)

Galliard (Matthew Carter, 1978)

Goudy Old Style (Frederic Goudy, 1915)

Granjon (George William Jones, 1928)

Hoefler Text (Jonathan Hoefler, 1991)

Minion (Robert Slimbach, 1990)

Palatino (Hermann Zapf, 1950)

Sabon (Jan Tschichold, 1966)

Weiss Roman (Emil Rudolf Weiss, 1926)

¶

Core Transitional Typeface:

Baskerville (1757)

John Baskerville (British, 1706–1775)

abcdefghijklmnop

qrstuvwxyz

ABCDEFGHIJK

LMNOPQRSTU

VWXYZ

0123456789

Type Designer Profile:

John Baskerville

(British, 1706–1775)

P. VIRGILII MARONIS

BUCOLICA

ECLOGA I. cui nomen *TITYRUS.*

MELIBOEUS, TITYRUS.

Tɪᴛʏʀᴇ, tu patulæ recubans fub tegmine fagi
Silveſtrem tenui Mufam meditaris avena:
Nos patriæ fines, et dulcia linquimus arva;
Nos patriam fugimus: tu, Tityre, lentus in umbra
5 Formofam refonare doces Amaryllida filvas.
T. O Meliboee, Deus nobis hæc otia fecit:
Namque erit ille mihi femper Deus: illius aram
Sæpe tener noſtris ab ovilibus imbuet agnus.
Ille meas errare boves, ut cernis, et ipfum
10 Ludere, quæ vellem, calamo permifit agrefti.
M. Non equidem invideo; miror magis: undique totis
Ufque adeo turbatur agris. en ipfe capellas
Protenus æger ago: hanc etiam vix, Tityre, duco:
Hic inter denfas corylos modo namque gemellos,
15 Spem gregis, ah! filice in nuda connixa reliquit.
Sæpe malum hoc nobis, fi mens non læva fuiſſet,
De cœlo taƈtas memini prædicere quercus:
Sæpe finiſtra cava prædixit ab ilice cornix.
Sed tamen, iſte Deus qui fit, da, Tityre, nobis.
20 *T.* Urbem, quam dicunt Romam, Meliboee, putavi
Stultus ego huic noſtræ fimilem, quo fæpe folemus
Paſtores ovium teneros depellere fœtus.
Sic canibus catulos fimiles, fic matribus hœdos
A   Noram;

Born in Worcestershire, England, John Baskerville moved to Birmingham in 1725, where he began working as a writing and stone-cutting master of gravestone inscriptions. In 1750, he set up his first printing press and soon realized that existing typefaces, substandard printing inks, and the technical limitations of the eighteenth-century printing press prevented him from meeting his own high book-production standards.

Up to this point in time, printed type lacked clarity and definition. The spread of ink on paper created heavier, softer letter-forms than their metal type counterparts. Baskerville modified his printing press to reproduce a lighter typographic impression, used denser and more concentrated inks for enhanced contrast and clarity, and introduced the use of hot-pressed "calendared" or wove paper that had a harder, crisper, less absorbent surface not previously available. These innovations provided him with finer results in the printing process, as well as a more pronounced visual contrast on the printed page (this also became an inherent design characteristic of his typefaces).

While Baskerville contributed significantly to eighteenth-century printing, he also was a true innovator in designing type. His typeface, Baskerville (1757; see page 29; right), possesses sharp, vertical proportions with stark contrasts between their thick and thin strokes. It is one of the few eighteenth-century typefaces successfully adapted to accommodate a wide range of technological advances.

His attention to fine detail and sensitivity to typographic nuances carried over into his romans, italics, large-scale capitals, small capitals, and old style numerals. It's also noticeable in his unorthodox use of judicious leading and letter spacing. While the typeface Baskerville remains one of the most distinctive and legible Transitional typefaces ever designed, most English printers continued to use Old Style typefaces such as Garamond (see page 22) throughout the eighteenth and nineteenth centuries. The typeface Baskerville was largely forgotten until Bruce Rogers (American, 1870–1957; see page 20) rediscovered it in 1917 and prompted several revivals.

Visual Characteristics:
Transitional

Stroke
**Weight contrast is more
pronounced than in Old
Style typefaces.**

Terminal
**Serifs are bracketed;
head serifs are oblique.**

Axis (or Stress)
**Curve letterforms have
a greater vertical, but
variable stress.**

Transitional

The Transitional type classification covers typefaces that transition from Old Style to Modern letterforms and first appeared in England and France in the mid-eighteenth century. The primary type influence on this group was the Romains du Roi (see page 34), designed by Phillippe Grandjean (French, 1666-1714) in 1702 for the French government's printing works or Imprimerie Royale.

The Romains du Roi marked a significant development in the history of typography. It was the first new typographic development that diverged from the Old Style genre prevalent throughout Europe during this time period, therefore it's identified as the first Transitional typeface.

Philippe Grandjean de Fouchy was born in 1666. As a young man in Paris, he visited a printing office by chance, which led him to design a set of type capitals. A member of the Royal Court saw Grandjean's early attempts, recommended him to Louis XIV, and subsequently he started working for the Imprimerie Royale.

In 1692, Louis XIV appointed a committee to draw up plans for a new typeface that would become the exclusive property of the government. The committee studied typefaces then in current use, historical manuscripts, and geometric principles. The outcome of this extensive study became the typeface Romains du Roi or "King's Roman." Grandjean was commissioned to design this new typeface, which took him eight years from 1694 until 1702, and ultimately established his reputation.

Revival Transitional Typeface:

Mrs. Eaves (1998)

Zuzana Licko (Czechoslovakian, b. 1961)

abcdefghijklmn

opqrstuvwxyz

ABCDEFGHIJ

KLMNOPQRS

TUVWXYZ

0123456789

Type Designer Profile:

Zuzana Licko

(Czechoslovakian, b. 1961)

Zuzana Licko is the cofounder of the Émigré type foundry and influential journal *Émigré Magazine*, together with her husband Rudy VanderLans (b. 1955). She immigrated to the United States in 1968, and graduated with a degree in graphic communications from the University of California, Berkeley in 1984.

In the mid-1980s, personal computers and low-resolution printers put the tools of typography in the hands of a broader public. In 1985, Licko began designing typefaces such as Emperor, Oakland, Émigré, and Universal (see above) that exploited the rough digital grain of early desktop systems. While other digital fonts imposed the coarse grid of screen displays and dot-matrix printers onto traditional typographic forms, Licko embraced this language. At the time, she and VanderLans called themselves "new primitives" and pioneers of a new technological dawn.

She also produced historical revivals alongside her experimental digital display typefaces. Licko's typeface Mrs. Eaves, inspired by the typefaces of John Baskerville (1706–1775; see page 30) (and named after his mistress Sarah Eaves), became one of the most popular typefaces of the 1990s.

Pierre Simon Fournier (French, 1712–1768), also known as Fournier le jeune, was the youngest son of the Fournier printing family. At an early age, he developed an interest in engraving woodblocks and large capitals before moving on to punch cutting and type design. In 1736, he established his own type foundry in Paris, where he designed more than 147 typefaces and typographical ornaments, and developed the idea of the type family. In 1737, he published the first version of his standardized system of type measurement—the point—and in 1742 published his first type specimen book.

Fournier's typefaces, including Fournier (1742) and Narcissus (1745), were influenced by the Romains du Roi and by the narrow proportioned letterforms predominantly used by printers and publishers in Holland and Germany at that time. Fournier designed one of the first early Transitional typefaces, St. Auguston Ordinaire, which served as the model for Monotype's Fournier, released in 1925.

Visual Characteristics

The distinguishing visual characteristics that separate Transitional typefaces from their Old Style predecessors are letterforms that are derived from geometry rather than hand-drawn forms, the introduction of a vertical stress in their curved letterforms, and sharper bracketed serifs that are less pronounced and subtler in profile. They are also characterized by a more pronounced contrast in stroke thickness, and a larger x-height defines their lowercase letters.

Transitional typefaces also possess more contrast in stroke variation which, was

Historical Influence:

Romains du Roi

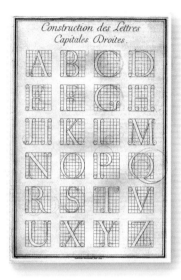

Romains du Roi was designed using a strict 48 by 48 square grid comprised of 2,304 modules. This system allowed Phillippe Grandjean (French, 1666-1714) to create an extensive family of letterforms with a unified consistency in their stroke contrast, weight, and serif profiles. Completed approximately fifty years later in 1745, the Romains du Roi type family was comprised of 86 fonts and marked a significant break from the Old Style typefaces of the period.

Grandjean's Romains du Roi (see above), also known as the "King's Roman" and the Paris Scientific Type, introduced groundbreaking graphic characteristics to his typeface that had never been utilized before. His horizontal serif with its unbracketed structure, as well as its extreme contrast in thick to thin strokes, was a counterpoint to the earlier humanist and calligraphic-inspired typefaces.

controversial at the time since it had an obvious and immediate impact on readability. This typographic detail was greatly influenced by improvements in printing technology, the introduction of hot-pressed papers, and improved printing inks.

These defining characteristics were precursors to the next typographic refinement with the Modern classification of typefaces.

Applications

Transitional typefaces are designed to function extremely well as large bodies of continuous book-scale text, as well as large-scale display settings. Additionally, the majority of typefaces within this classification possess a visual cohesiveness since their italic equivalents have been designed as integral parts of their typographic families.

These characteristics provide a graphic designer with a broader palette of options for creating visual emphasis and differentiation than with the italics of earlier Garalde or Humanist typefaces.

Seminal Transitional Typefaces:
Bell (Richard Austin, 1788)
Bulmer (William Martin, 1792)
Caledonia (William Addison Dwiggins, 1938)
Caslon (William Caslon, 1725)
Electra (William Addison Dwiggins, 1935)
Fournier (Pierre Simon Fournier, 1742)
Meridien (Adrian Fruitger, 1957)
Perpetua (Arthur Eric Rowton Gill, 1928)
Plantin (Frank Hinman Pierpont, 1913)
Spectrum (Jan van Krimpen, 1957)
Stone Serif (Sumner Stone, 1987)
Times New Roman (Stanley Morison, 1932)
¶

Core Modern Typeface:

Bodoni (1798)

Giambattista Bodoni (Italian, 1740–1813)

abcdefghijklmnop

pqrstuvwxyz

ABCDEFGHIJKL

MNOPQRSTU

VWXYZ

0123456789

Type Designer Profile:

Giambattista Bodoni

(Italian, 1740–1813)

In the late 1800s, Giambattista Bodoni was one of the most renowned punch cutters, type designers, and printers in Europe and the creator of one of the first Modern typefaces. Known as the "King of Printers," he was born the son of a printer in 1740 in northern Italy. At age eighteen, he worked as a compositor for Propaganda Fide in Rome and then became director of the Duke of Parma's printing press at the age of twenty-eight.

Typefaces created during this same time period by designers Pierre Simon Fournier (French, 1712–1768) and Firmin Didot (French, 1764–1836) influenced Bodoni's work. He used them as his primary references in developing his typeface Bodoni in 1798. It was one of the first Modern typefaces to exhibit extreme contrasts of light and dark in its thick and thin strokes, as well as to have a vertical stress and razor-sharp serifs with unsupported brackets. During his lifetime, Bodoni also designed numerous script typefaces.

Bodoni documented his philosophy and principles of typography in his *Manuale Tipografico* (1816; see above), which reveals his innovative use of large-scale type, generous white space on the page, and minimal page ornamentation.

Bodoni's typefaces were considered radical and somewhat abstract at the time of their introduction. Thin, straight serifs, vertical axis, and extreme contrast from thick to thin strokes were all radical departures from the visual characteristics of the earlier Transitional typefaces.

Modern

The Modern classification of typefaces, also known as Didone, is based upon typefaces produced in the late-eighteenth and early-nineteenth centuries in Italy by Giambattista Bodoni (Italian, 1740–1813) and in France by Firmin Didot (French, 1764–1836).

Moderns are characterized by a pronounced contrast in weight between the vertical strokes and the horizontal hairlines, which serves to emphasize the vertical stress of the letters. These visual qualities allow for extended families, incorporating a range of widths and weights, including both extended, ultra bolds, and condensed typefaces.

Bodoni was a prolific type designer responsible for hundreds of typefaces. The Museo Bodoniano houses more than 25,000 of his type punches, and his *Manuale*

Visual Characteristics:
Modern

Stroke
Contrast between thick
and thin strokes is
abrupt and dramatic.

Terminal
Stroke terminals are
ball shapes, with thin, flat,
unbracketed serifs.

Axis (or Stress)
Axis of curved strokes
is vertical with little or
no bracketing.

Tipografico, published in 1818, contains over 140 roman typefaces with their corresponding italics.

The Didot family of Paris was involved in every aspect of publishing, printing, type design, punch cutting, and paper manufacturing during the late-eighteenth and early-nineteenth centuries. Firmin Didot, grandson of the founder, is historically known as the most important member of this family because he is commonly thought to have produced the first Modern typeface in 1784.

In 1783, at the age of nineteen, Didot took control of his father's type foundry. The following year, he produced the first Modern typeface characterized by thin slab-like, unbracketed serifs, a marked vertical stress, and an abrupt transition from thick to thin strokes. During this same time period, the

Didots began reproducing these typographic details for the first time by using wove paper and an improved printing press. As a result of these innovative developments, Didot became the prevalent book typeface used throughout France during the nineteenth century. It is still in use today.

Visual Characteristics

The most prominent visual characteristics of Modern typeface are their extreme and abrupt contrast in stroke weights; fine, thinner strokes appear as a hairline weight while the heavier strokes are thick and exaggerated in comparison. Serifs are thin and completely flat, with little if any bracketing. The stress axis of Modern characters is almost invariably vertical with little or no bracketing. Letterform apertures are very tight; and in many

abcdefghijklmnop

qrstuvwxyz

ABCDEFGHIJKL

MNOPQRSTUVW

XYZ

0123456789

Type Designer Profile:

Aldo Novarese

(Italian, 1920–1998)

Aldo Novarese was one of the modern era's most prolific type designers. He attended the Turin School of Printing, where he studied woodcarving, etching, and lithography. After working as a graphic arts teacher, he joined the Nebiolo Type Foundry, where he ultimately became the foundry's art director in 1952.

He collaborated with Allesandro Butti (Italian, 1893–1959) on many of his early typefaces including Augustea (1951) and Microgramma (1952), which, with the addition of its lowercase, became Eurostile in 1962. In 1980, Novarese designed the type that bears his name, Novarese, for the Haas Type Foundry.

Novarese is also well known as the author of *Alfabeta: Lo Studio e il Disegno del Carattere* (1964; see above), a book about the origins and evolution of typefaces in history.

Image: Torino Progresso Grafico ©1946.

examples stroke terminals are ball-shaped. While the width of most Modern uppercase letterforms is regularized; wide letterforms such as the "M" and "W" are condensed while others such as the "P" and "T" are expanded.

Applications

Modern typefaces are mostly used for large-scale titling and display purposes, which emphasizes the elegance of their individual characters. Their extreme stroke contrasts create dynamic and bold visual effects; however, these extreme stroke contrasts limit readability and legibility at smaller, text-size settings.

Additional leading, kerning, generous margins, and ample white space are required to enhance readability and legibility of Modern typefaces.

Seminal Modern Typefaces:

Arepo (Sumner Stone, 1995)
Centennial (Adrian Frutiger, 1986)
Craw Modern (Freeman Craw, 1958)
Didot (Firmin Didot, 1799)
HTF Didot (Jonathan Hoefler, 1991)
Marconi (Hermann Zapf, 1976)
Melior (Hermann Zapf, 1952)
Modern No. 216 (Edward Benguiat, 1982)
Torino (Allesandro Butti, 1908)
Walbaum (Justis Erich Walbaum, 1800)
¶

Core Slab Serif Typeface:

Clarendon (1845)

Robert Besley (British, 1794–1876) with Benjamin Fox (British, d. 1877)

abcdefghijklmn

opqrstuvwxyz

ABCDEFGHIJ

KLMNOPQRS

TUVWXYZ

0123456789

Type Designer Profile:

Robert Besley

(British, 1794–1876)

Robert Besley worked for the Fann Street Foundry in London as a punch cutter and type designer from 1840 to 1860. In 1845, he created the typeface Clarendon, initially described as a "fat typeface with thick slabs" which marked a significant transition from traditional slab serif Antiques and Egyptians that were popular during the late-nineteenth century to typefaces with bracketed serifs. It was the prototype slab serif that was equally effective in text settings where emphasis was needed, as well as for large-scale display needs such as advertisements, posters, broadsides, and signs.

Named after Oxford University's Clarendon Press, this popular slab-serif typeface was the first registered typeface and one of the last new typographic developments of the nineteenth century. The example shown above is a detail from Robert Besley's type specimen catalog.

Slab Serif

Until the beginning of the nineteenth century, the majority of type served one sole purpose—for book-scale text settings. As industrial innovation took hold, the need for new means of communication to the public were needed—newspapers, advertisements, posters, billboards, and signs all required a new form of typography. It was due to these new needs that the display typeface was born.

Slab Serifs, also known as Antiques, Egyptians, Geometrics, or Clarendons, were introduced at the onset of the Industrial Revolution in England and were the first display typefaces specifically designed for these new large-scale display needs.

The first Slab Serif typefaces were designed by the influential type founder Vincent Figgins (British, 1766–1844) in the early nineteenth century. Introduced as Antiques in 1815, these typefaces were completely monotone in weight, including their serifs, which were unbracketed and available only in capitals. Later refined versions included lowercase and bracketed serifs and were identified as Egyptians. Finally, in the mid-nineteenth century, versions with the same differentiation in stroke weights, called Clarendons, were introduced.

The design of Slab Serif typefaces during the twentieth century reflects a wide range of historical and technological influences. For example, some contemporary Slab Serifs are clearly derived from Modern typefaces where others are clearly direct descendants of early Sans Serif Grotesques.

An exceptional twenty-first century Slab Serif typeface is Archer (Jonathan Hoefler, 2001). This diverse typeface family is available

---

Slab Serif

Y d r O

Stroke
Slight stroke contrast or generally imperceptible changes in stroke weight.

Letterform
Short ascenders and descenders.

Terminal
Stroke terminals are short to medium length serifs or very heavy serifs with little or no bracketing.

Axis (or Stress)
Axis of curved strokes is vertical.

in numerous weights and italics, and is as effective in extensive text settings as it is for large-scale display purposes. Originally designed for *Martha Stewart Living* magazine, Archer has clear visual cues to typewriter-based slab serif typefaces, with distinctive nuances such as ball terminals.

Slab Serif typefaces are also identified as Ionics, Mécanes, or Mechanicals.

Visual Characteristics
Slab Serif typefaces have moderate to minimal contrast in stroke weights, sometimes appearing completely monotone. Their serifs are bracketed or unbracketed, short to medium in length, the same weight as their letterform stems, and either square or rectangular in profile. The stress axis of Slab Serif characters is almost invariably vertical.

This classification includes both Slab Serif typefaces with bracketed serifs, also identified as Clarendons or Ionics, and typefaces with square or unbracketed serifs, identified as Egyptians.

Applications
Slab Serif typefaces were initially developed from large-scale display letters used in both woodblock letterpress printing and architectural lettering.

They are designed to function most effectively when used in text settings where heavier weights are required. Their strong and apparent serifs, as well as their consistent stroke widths, are easily retained when printed on rough or absorbent paper stocks, such as newsprint for newspaper production. They also retain their typographic

Revival Slab Serif Typeface:

Archer (2001)

Jonathan Hoefler (American, b. 1970)

abcdefghijklmno

pqrstuvwxyz

ABCDEFGHIJK

LMNOPQRSTU

VWXYZ

0123456789

Type Designer Profile:
Jonathan Hoefler
(American, b. 1970)

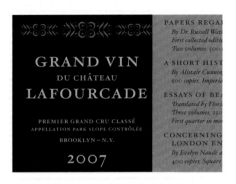

Jonathan Hoefler is a type designer and type historian who specializes in designing original typefaces. He established Hoefler Type Foundry in 1989.

Named one of the forty most influential designers in America by *I.D. Magazine*, his work includes award-winning original type-faces for *Rolling Stone, Harper's Bazaar, The New York Times Magazine, Sports Illustrated,* and *Esquire.* His institutional clients range from the Solomon R. Guggenheim Museum in New York City to the rock band They Might Be Giants.

Hoefler's best-known work is the Hoefler Text family of typefaces (see above), designed for Apple Computer, Inc. and now part of the Macintosh operating system. His work has been exhibited internationally, and is included in the permanent design collections of the Smithsonian's Cooper-Hewitt National Design Museum and the Museum of Modern Art (MoMA) in New York City.

In 2002, The Association Typographique Internationale (ATypI) presented Hoefler with its most prestigious award, the Prix Charles Peignot for outstanding contribu-tions to type design.

Image: Hoefler & Co. ©1991.

character and clarity when reversed out of a dark background which makes them extremely well-suited for large-scale display purposes.

Slab Serifs, especially Clarendons, were used extensively throughout the 1950s and 1960s in publishing, packaging, and editorial design due to these diverse visual characteristics. Additionally, they were often used in typewriters which gave way to Courier (Susan Nobrega, 1955) becoming one of the most ubiquitous Slab Serifs of the mid- to late-twentieth century. Today it is one of numerous monospace digital text typefaces used for computer and programming tech-nologies since its rigorous spacing system ensures consistent letter spacing between letterform and the pixel-based grid of a display screen.

Seminal Slab Serif Typefaces:

American Typewriter (Joel Kaden, Tony Stan, 1974)

Beton (Heinrich Jost, 1931)

Bookman (Edward Benguiat, 1975)

Century Schoolbook (Morris Fuller Benton, 1924)

Cheltenham (Bertram Grosvenor Goodhue, 1896)

City (Georg Trump, 1930)

Excelsior (Chauncey Griffith, 1931)

Lubalin Graph (Herb Lubalin, 1974)

Memphis (Emil Rudolf Weiss, 1929)

Playbill (Robert Harling, 1938)

Rockwell (Frank Hinman Pierpont, 1934)

Sentinel (Jonathan Hoefler, Tobias Frere-Jones, 2009)

Serifa (Adrian Frutiger, 1967)

Stymie (Morris Fuller Benton, 1931)

¶

Sans Serif (Grotesque, Neo-Grotesque, Geometric, Humanist)

The type classification Sans Serif includes all typefaces without serifs, identified either as Sans Serif, Gothic, or Grotesque. In this context, this type classification is organized in four (4) subcategories: Grotesque, Neo-Grotesque, Geometric, and Humanist.

The earliest known Sans Serif letterforms were Greek Ionic carved inscriptions, dating back to as early as the fifth century BCE. These were later used as inspiration by twentieth-century type designers such as Carol Twombly (American, b. 1959; see page 73) for her Sans Serif Glyphic typeface Lithos (1989; see page 73).

The first Sans Serif typeface was a set of monoline capital letterforms shown above, designed by William Caslon IV (British, 1780–1869) in 1816. The term "sans surryph" was first used in 1833 and ultimately became known as Sans (French for "without") Serif. These typefaces first gained popularity in Western Europe in the nineteenth century.

Stroke weight is even and uniform with little or no contrast between thick and thin strokes, and their stress is almost always vertical. The italic versions of Sans Serif typefaces often appear as slanted romans or obliques. Franklin Gothic, Futura, and Univers are all classified as Sans Serif typefaces.

Core Sans Serif Grotesque Typeface:
Franklin Gothic (1903)
Morris Fuller Benton (American, 1872–1948)

abcdefghijklmno

pqrstuvwxyz

ABCDEFGHIJKLM

NOPQRSTUVW

XYZ

0123456789

Type Designer Profile:

Morris Fuller Benton

(American, 1872–1948)

ABCDEFGHIJKL
MNOPQRSTUV
WXYZ& $12345
67890·AKMNS

Morris Fuller Benton · 1935 · Specimen

HARDWARE
MATERIALS FOR CONTRACTORS AND MECHANICS

FARMING AND FACTORY
SUPPLIES

TRACTOR AND AUTOMOBILE
SERVICE STATION

STEPHENER & BUSHSTEIN
OFFICE AND DELIVERY YARD
RUNSDEN CENTER, MAINE

Morris Fuller Benton was one of the most prolific American type designers during the first half of the twentieth century. Benton's father, Linn Boyd Benton (American, 1844–1932), was director of the American Type Founders (ATF) design department. There Morris Fuller became his father's assistant and learned every aspect of type founding and design.

As director of the ATF design department from 1900 to 1937, he designed 221 typefaces, ranging from historic revivals and original typefaces to his large family of Sans Serif Grotesques, known as Gothics (see above), plus eighteen variations on the typeface Century (1924), including the popular Century Schoolbook (1918). Benton also worked closely with Henry Lewis Bullen (American, 1857–1938), collector of ATF's famous type library and mentor of type publicist and typographic scholar Beatrice Warde (American, 1900–1969).

Sans Serif Grotesque

Grotesques, also known as Gothics, are classified as Sans Serif typefaces that originated in the nineteenth century. The prolific American type designer Morris Fuller Benton was responsible for two of the most timeless Sans Serif Grotesques designed in the early twentieth century—Franklin Gothic (1903) and News Gothic (1908). Both typefaces possess a wide range of weights and styles providing a diverse range of uses, working as effectively in small-scale text settings or as in large-scale display.

Sans Serif Grotesque

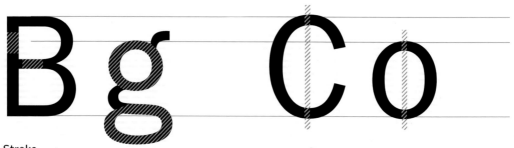

Stroke
**Obvious contrast in
stroke weight; slightly
"squared" profile to
the curves; bowl-and-
loop lowercase "g" in
many versions.**

Axis (Or Stress)
**Axis of curved strokes
is vertical.**

In the 1930s, a family of standardized Grotesque-based typefaces were developed in Germany as the official typeface for the state. Known as Din, referring to the Deutsche Industrie-Norm (or German Industrial Standard), these typefaces were used extensively and consistently for all road and traffic signs throughout the German Republic. In the 1990s, Albert-Jan Pool (Dutch, b. 1960; see page 49) redesigned the typeface family, which now includes an extensive set of weights, italics, width, sizes, and alternate characters. The new FF Din typeface family was released in 1995 under the FontFont label.

Visual Characteristics

The most prominent visual characteristics of Sans Serif Grotesque typefaces are that they possess a noticeable contrast between thick and thin strokes, and their terminals are usually horizontal. In some typefaces, the capital "G" has a spur and the capital "R" has a curled leg.

The most distinguishing characteristic of Grotesque typefaces is their bowl and loop lowercase "g" and a more obvious, monotone weight stress than their Sans Serif counterparts.

Applications

In the late-nineteenth and early-twentieth centuries, Sans Serif Grotesques were primarily used for large-scale display applications such as signwriting and architectural lettering. These early Grotesques were initially designed with only capital letterforms that possessed uneven stroke weight and irregular curvilinear letter profiles.

Revival Sans Serif Grotesque Typeface:

FF Din (1995)

Albert-Jan Pool (Dutch, b. 1960)

abcdefghijklmnop

qrstuvwxyz

ABCDEFGHIJKLM

NOPQRSTUVW

XYZ

0123456789

Type Designer Profile:

Albert-Jan Pool (Dutch, b. 1960)

Albert-Jan Pool is a Dutch type designer based in Hamburg, Germany.

He studied graphic design and type design with type designer and author Gerrit Noordzij (Dutch, b. 1950) at the Royal Academy of Art in The Hague. Since 1994, he has run his own design studio, Dutch Design, where he continues to design typefaces for clients including FontFont, Jet/Conoco, C&A, and HEM/Tamoil.

He wrote and designed *Branding with Type* (with coauthors Stefan Rögener and Ursula Packhäuser) on the effects of typography on brand image, published by Adobe Press in 1995. He is a professor at the Muthesius Academy in Kiel, where he teaches type design at the undergraduate and graduate levels.

In 2010, the Museum of Modern Art (MoMA) included Pool's typeface FF DIN in its first set of acquired digital typefaces for the institution's design collection. FF Din is used extensively and consistently for all road and traffic signs throughout the German Republic (see above).

As further refinements were incorporated in the later Grotesques, they were able to balance function with visual appeal and were used for a wide range of applications including display typography, environmental graphics, and architectural signs.

While many early Grotesques have a smaller x-height, the majority of these typefaces work well for smaller-scale text settings, as well as for large-scale display needs.

Seminal Sans Serif Grotesque Typefaces:

Alternate Gothic (Morris Fuller Benton, 1903)

Bureau Grotesque (David Berlow, 1989)

Champion (Jonathan Hoefler, 1990)

Knockout (Jonathan Hoefler,
        Tobias Frere-Jones, 1994)

News Gothic (Morris Fuller Benton, 1908)

Trade Gothic (Jackson Burke, 1948)
¶

Core Sans Serif Neo-Grotesque Typeface:
Helvetica (1956)
Max Miedinger (Swiss, 1910–1980)

abcdefghijklmnop

qrstuvwxyz

ABCDEFGHIJKL

MNOPQRSTUVW

XYZ

0123456789

Type Designer Profile:

Max Miedinger

(Swiss, 1910–1980)

Max Miedinger was born in 1910 in Zurich, Switzerland. Between 1926 and 1930, Miedinger trained as a typesetter and graphic designer while attending evening classes at the Kunstgewerbeschule (School of Applied Arts).

In the early 1950s, he became an in-house type designer with Haas Type Foundry in Münchenstein, Switzerland, where he designed his most famous typeface, Helvetica (see right), in 1956; it is the most widely used Sans Serif Neo-Grotesque in the world.

It was at Haas where its director, Eduard Hoffmann (Swiss, 1892–1980), asked Miedinger to adapt the foundry's existing Haas Grotesk to accommodate current taste. Haas Grotesk had its origins in nineteenth-century German work such as Berthold's Akizidenz Grotesk (1896). The new typeface, created from Miedinger's china-ink drawings, was a new design in its own right rather than one with minor modifications, as had been the original plan. Neue Haas Grotesk, as it was originally called, proved extremely popular. When D. Stempel AG in Germany released the typeface in 1961, the foundry called it Helvetica, the traditional Latin name for "Switzerland," to capitalize on the increasing popularity of Swiss School and the International Typographic Style. Although not planned as a diverse family of weights like Adrian Frutiger's Univers (1954, see pages 54, 137), Helvetica has been added to during the past thirty years, and is available on most typesetting systems.

Sans Serif Neo-Grotesque

This type classification includes the second generation of Sans Serif Grotesque type-faces that were designed starting in the 1950s, influenced by the emergence of the International Typographic Style, also known as the Swiss School.

The International Typographic Style was defined by the use of Neo-Grotesque typefaces and employed a rigorous page grid that produced asymmetrical layouts. Its philosophy evolved directly from the de Stijl Movement, the Bauhaus, and Jan Tschichold's *The New Typography* (see page 27). This groundbreaking movement helped spread the International Typographic Style, which became a major modernist design influence throughout Europe and the United States during the latter part of the twentieth century.

Visual Characteristics:
Sans Serif Neo-Grotesque

Axis
**Axis of curved strokes
is vertical.**

Letterform
**High x-height; open
stroke to lowercase "g;"
less contrast to stroke,
more uniform.**

The typographic genesis of this movement was Akzidenz Grotesk (1896), produced by the Berthold Foundry. It became a favored typeface among typographers and graphic designers of the Swiss International Typographic Style and, more importantly, became a visual benchmark for Max Miedinger's development of Neue Haas Grotesk (later renamed Helvetica in 1961; see page 51).

Both typefaces are emblematic of this type classification; each possesses an innocuous, mechanical appearance with little or no visual character. However, they both exemplify the intentions of the modernist movement, where typography needed to be a neutral vehicle of meaning. Neo-Grotesque typefaces cannot be traced to any particular region of the world or culture other than having a strong association with the modernist design principles of the time period in which they were developed.

The visual distinctions between Akzidenz Grotesk and Helvetica are evident in the latter's taller x-height and slightly narrower proportion, with both of these characteristics making Helvetica a more practical and functional typeface for a variety of applications.

Visual Characteristics

Neo-Grotesque typefaces, also identified as Transitionals or Realists, include many of the Sans Serif typefaces used today.

As their name implies, Neo-Grotesque typefaces are much more refined than their earlier Grotesque counterparts. These refinements include minimal stroke contrast, a noticeably higher x-height, closed apertures,

Contemporary Influence:

Univers

					39 univers

45 univers	46 *univers*	47 univers	48 *univers*	49 univers

53 univers	55 univers	56 *univers*	57 univers	58 *univers*	59 univers

63 univers	65 univers	66 *univers*	67 univers	68 *univers*

73 **univers**	75 **univers**	76 ***univers***

83 **univers**

Adrian Frutiger (Swiss, 1928–2015), one of the most prominent type designers of the twentieth century, was responsible for one of the most notable typeface families ever to be created—the Neo-Grotesque typeface Univers.

The twenty-one variations of the Univers typeface family have five weights and four widths. At its center is Univers 55, the equivalent of a standard "book" weight typeface. Frutiger abandoned imprecise terms such as "condensed," "extended," "light," "bold," "roman," and "italic," and instead used a reference numbering system that illustrated the proportional relationships between each typeface variation. At the time, it was a revolutionary concept for how typefaces and their related families could be described.

He also created a visual "periodic table" (see above; page 54) for the Univers family—its vertical axis identifies different weights; any variation beginning with the same number is of the same weight. Its horizontal axis identifies profile shifts; from extended to condensed with italic variations. Any weight ending with an even number is italic. Roman variations are designated with an odd number; oblique variations with an even number.

The Univers family of typefaces is known for its remarkable visual uniformity, which enables any graphic designer to use all twenty-one fonts together as a flexible, integrated typographic system.

Revival Sans Serif Neo-Grotesque Typeface:

Bell Centennial (1978)

Matthew Carter (British, b. 1937)

abcdefghijklmnopq

stuvwxyz

ABCDEFGHIJKLMN

OPQRSTUVWXYZ

0123456789

Matthew Carter

(British, b. 1937)

MANTINIA · MCMXCIII
CAPS AᴬBᴮCᶜDᴰEᴱFᶠGᴳHᴴ
AND IᴵJᴶKᴷLᴸMᴹNᴺOᴼPQℚ
SUPERIOR RᴿSˢTTᵁUᵛW
CAPˢ WᵂXˣYʸ&&ZZᴁᴁᴁᴁ
FIGURES 1234567890
SMALᴸ•CAPˢ ACEHIORSTUWZ
LIGATUREˢ TH VCT HE UP LA
TT CT TU TW TY ME MP MD MB 'E
ALˈERNATIVES T&Y Rᴿ QQ

Matthew Carter is an English-born American type designer and type scholar based in Cambridge, Massachusetts.

In 1956, Carter spent a year studying the traditional crafts of type design and type founding with Jan Van Krimpen's (Dutch, 1892–1958) assistant, the punch cutter P. H. Raidische, at the Enschede Font Foundry in Holland.

For the past fifty years, Carter has designed and produced type (such as the revival Old Style typeface Mantinia (1993) shown above) in every possible medium, from metal to film and digital. Prior to starting his own digital type foundry, Carter & Cone Type, Inc. in 1991, he worked for Mergenthaler Linotype and Bitstream.

He has received the Chrysler Award for Innovation in Design, the Type Directors Club Medal, and the American Institute of Graphic Arts Medal. In 1981, London's Royal Society of Arts elected him a Royal Designer for Industry. Carter was named a MacArthur Foundation Fellow in 2011.

circular letterforms, and horizontal terminals. Typefaces in this classification also offer a broader range of widths and weight to meet new production needs in phototypesetting, printing, and digital media.

Applications

Neo-Grotesque typefaces function more effectively in small text-size settings than any other Sans Serif classification due to their ample x-height and well-proportioned counters. These two factors further ensure layout economy, legibility, and readability in most applications.

Many typefaces in this type classification offer extensive type families with a wide range of weights, condensed and expanded versions, and outlines, as well as versions with rounded terminals. This diversity makes Neo-Grotesque typefaces particularly well-suited for a range of applications, from book-scale text settings to large-scale display needs.

Seminal Sans Serif Neo-Grotesque Typefaces:
Akzidenz Grotesk (1896)
Folio (Walter Baum, Konrad Friedrich Bauer, 1957)
Univers (Adrian Frutiger, 1976)
Bell Gothic (Chauncey H. Griffith, 1938)
¶

Core Sans Serif Geometric Typeface:
Futura (1927)
Paul Renner (German, 1878–1956)

abcdefghijklmnopq

rstuvwxyz

ABCDEFGHIJKLM

NOPQRSTUVW

XYZ

0123456789

Paul Renner

Paul Renner was a German typographer, graphic designer, and educator best known as the designer of Futura, a groundbreaking Sans Serif Geometric typographic landmark of modernist form still popular today. His original design included a set of alternative characters (see above) that was unpopular with most end users.

During the 1920s and 1930s, he was a prominent member of the Deutscher Werkbund (German Work Federation). As an author, he fashioned a new set of visual guidelines for balanced book design in his books *Typografie als Kunst* (1922, translated "Typography as Art") and *Die Kunst der Typographie* (1953, translated as "The Art of Typography").

Renner established the Meisterschule für Deutchlands Buchdrucher (Advanced School of German Bookprinting) in Munich. In 1937, Renner was removed from his post by the Nazis for "subversive typography."

Sans Serif Geometric

This subcategory of Sans Serif typefaces reflects the twentieth-century ideology of modernism that swept through Europe and the United States from the 1930s to the 1950s. These typefaces were developed to reflect the simplicity of pure geometric form and are void of any historical reference and past tradition.

Sans Serif Geometric typefaces are constructed from pure geometric shapes and proportions, as opposed to being derived from earlier Grotesques (see page 47) or Neo-Grotesques (see page 52), or from the calligraphic influences of Humanist (see page 64) typefaces. Their monoline letterforms have circular bowls and share many geometric components.

The first Geometric, Erbar-Grotesk (1908), is credited to type designer Jakob Erbar (German, 1878–1935). It was originally intended to be used as a highly legible typeface, but due to its rigid adherence to the circle, it was only suitable for display purposes. Erbar was subsequently used by Paul Renner as a study model for the development of his Futura typeface.

Futura (1927, see page 57), deemed the first "modern" Geometric, was designed by type designer Paul Renner (German, 1878-1956). This typeface was initially developed as Renner's interpretation of the New Typography and quickly became a twentieth century classic. It is a timeless representation

Visual Characteristics:
Sans Serif Geometric

ER ad O

Stroke
Strokes are strict monolines with no contrast.

Letterform
Geometric forms evident in most character shapes and profiles.

Axis
Axis of curved strokes is vertical.

of a functional modern typeface because it maintains visual consistency, readability, and legibility across an extended family of sizes and weights.

Kabel (1927), designed by type designer Rudolf Koch (German, 1876–1934) for the Klingspor Type Foundry, reflects a slightly more Humanistic nuance than Futura or the later Avant Garde. For example, traditional roman letterform profiles are clearly evident in Kabel's lowercase "a," "g," and "t." Additionally, the angled cross bar of the lowercase "e" alludes to early Venetian or Humanist letterforms (see page 17).

Avant Garde (1970) by type designer Herb Lubalin (American, 1918–1981) was originally designed as a display face while he was art director for the magazine of the same name. This rigorous and dramatic Geometric

typeface is comprised of an extensive range of capital ligatures that allow for tight settings that were a prevalent visual element of the magazine's design.

Sans Serif Geometric typefaces also include typefaces constructed solely on a square module and where the use of curved strokes is minimized or eliminated. These typefaces, such as Morris Sans (Morris Fuller Benton, 1930), Eurostile (Aldo Novarese, 1962), Microgramma (Aldo Novarese, 1952), and Bourgeois (Jonathan Barnbrook, 2005), have limited applications and are predominantly used for display purposes.

One of the most widely-used Geometrics of the twenty-first century is Gotham (Tobias Frere-Jones, 2000, see page 61). Its genesis was inspired by post-war building lettering and hand-painted signs popular in New

Contemporary Influence:

Herbert Bayer's Universal

Modernist graphic designer Herbert Bayer's (Austrian, 1900-1985) Universal (1925) "idealist" typeface is emblematic of the Sans Serif Geometric classification; a fact that is further reinforced by its integral appearance on the façade of the Bauhaus building (see above) in Dessau, Germany.

In 1921, Bayer enrolled as a student at the Bauhaus in Weimar where he studied under Wassily Kandinsky (Russian, 1866-1944) and later, under László Moholy-Nagy (Hungarian, 1895-1946). Following the closing of the Bauhaus in Weimar, arrangements were made to transfer the school to Dessau, and in 1925 Bayer and five other former students, including Marcel Breuer (Hungarian, 1902–1981), Joost Schmidt (German, 1893-1948), and Josef Albers (German, 1888-1976), were appointed teachers.

As an educator, Bayer transformed the Bauhaus by eliminating the use of lithography and woodcuts and introducing movable type and mechanical presses to the Dessau workshops. The use of serif, blackletter, and capital letterforms ended; the use of Sans Serif and lowercase letterforms began. Typographic form was now asymmetric, simple, and direct.

This monoline typeface initially designed without capital letterforms, is composed entirely of pure geometric shapes—straight lines, circles, and arcs. Universal has influenced numerous twentieth and twenty-first century type designers in pursuit of pure geometric typographic form.

Bayer left the Bauhaus in 1928 and relocated to Berlin. In 1938, like many artists and designers in Germany at the time, he fled the Nazis and immigrated to the United States where he became a self-appointed spokesperson for the Bauhaus movement.

Image: Peter Drews ©2011.

Revival Sans Serif Geometric Typeface:

Gotham (2000)
Tobias Frere-Jones (American, b. 1970)

abcdefghijklmn
opqrstuvwxyz
ABCDEFGHIJK
LMNOPQRSTU
VWXYZ
0123456789

Type Designer Profile:

Tobias Frere-Jones

(American, b. 1970)

For over 25 years, Tobias Frere-Jones has established himself as one of the world's leading type designers, creating some of the most widely used typefaces available today, including Interstate (1999), Poynter (1997), Whitney (2004), Surveyor (2001), Tungsten (2009), Retina (2000), and Gotham (2000).

Frere-Jones's design of Gotham, which he also identifies as an American "working class" typeface, was influenced by signs and lettering evident in the post-war buildings of New York City (see above).

Tobias studied graphic design at the Rhode Island School of Design graduating in 1992. He joined the faculty of the Yale University School of Art in 1996 and has lectured throughout the United States, Europe, and Australia. His work is in the permanent collections of the Victoria & Albert Museum (V&A) in London and the Museum of Modern Art (MoMA) in New York. In 2006, The Royal Academy of Visual Arts in The Hague (KABK) awarded him the Gerrit Noordzij Prijs for his contributions to typographic design, writing, and education.

In 2013, he received the AIGA Medal, in recognition of exceptional achievements in the field of design.

Image: Hoefler & Co. ©2000.

York City during the mid-twentieth century. Gotham is an extensive type family of four widths and eight weights, with a separate font design for screen display purposes. It possesses strong geometric profiles, a high x-height, and wide apertures.

Visual Characteristics

Sans Serif Geometric typefaces are built from simple geometric shapes and proportions, such as circles and squares, and maintain a strict monoline appearance. They have little to no stroke contrast and sometimes feature a single-story lowercase "a."

The typefaces within this type classification are among the least legible of Sans Serif typefaces and are usually only suitable for large-scale titling and display purposes.

Applications

While there are a few exceptions, the majority of Sans Serif Geometric typefaces do not function very effectively when used in extensive small-scale text settings. Due to their integral and rigorous geometric profiles, they are better suited for large-scale display purposes.

Seminal Sans Serif Geometric Typefaces:
Avant Garde (Herb Lubalin, 1970)
Bourgeois (Jonathan Barnbrook, 2005)
Erbar (Jakob Erbar, 1922)
Eurostile (Aldo Novarese, 1962)
Kabel (Rudolf Koch, 1927)
Metro (William Addison Dwiggins, 1929)
Morris Sans (Morris Fuller Benton, 1930)
Universal (Herbert Bayer, 1925)
¶

Core Sans Serif Humanist Typeface:

Gill Sans (1927)

Arthur Eric Rowton Gill (British, 1882–1940)

abcdefghijklmnopq

rstuvwxyz

ABCDEFGHIJKLM

NOPQRSTUVW

XYZ

0123456789

Type Designer Profile:

Arthur Eric Rowton Gill

(British, 1882–1940)

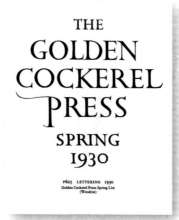

Eric Gill was a prominent English letter cutter, sculptor, wood engraver, and type designer. He was born in 1882 in Brighton and studied at the Chichester Art School before becoming an apprentice to a London architect. While working in London, he attended classes taught by calligrapher Edward Johnston (Uruguayan, 1872–1944) at the Central School of Arts and Crafts, launching him into a career as a stonecutter and letterer.

Gill designed his first typeface, Perpetua, in 1925 for typographer Stanley Morison (British, 1889–1967), typographic advisor for Monotype Corporation. Perpetua takes its name from the first book in which it was used (in its first size), *The Passion of Perpetua and Felicity*. The original italic version, cut in 1930, was called Felicity, but is not the same as the Perpetua italic finally released.

Gill Sans (1927), designed during the same time period, was conceived as a Sans Serif Humanist text typeface, in comparison to New Johnston (1916) designed by Edward Johnston, specifically developed for the London Underground sign system.

In addition to his typographic work, Gill designed catalogs and limited editions of classic works that included his original wood engravings for Golden Cockerel Press (est. 1920; see above).

In 1935, Gill became an Associate of the Royal Institute of British Architects and an Associate of the Royal Academy. In 1936, Gill was part of the first group of individuals to receive the title "Royal Designer of Industry."

Sans Serif Humanist

Sans Serif typefaces in the Humanist type classification are based upon the integral relationships and proportions of roman inscriptional letterforms and possess a strong calligraphic influence.

One of the most influential and timeless Humanist typefaces of the twentieth century is Gill Sans (Arthur Eric Rowton Gill, 1927; see page 63) which was itself influenced by a typeface designed by Edward Johnston (Uruguayan, 1872–1944) for the London Underground in 1916. Both designers came from a lettering craft background; Johnston was a calligrapher; Gill was a sculptor and letter carver. Both typefaces reflect a strong and obvious visual relationship to the proportions of classical Roman letterforms.

This preeminent monoline typeface also influenced subsequent developments within the Humanist type genre. This is evident in numerous typefaces that have been designed throughout the twentieth and early twenty-first centuries.

Visual Characteristics:
Sans Serif Humanist

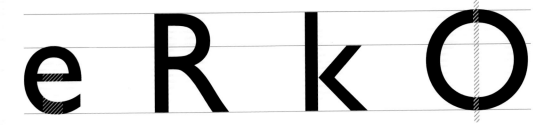

Stroke
Visually apparent contrast in stroke weights.

Letterform
Based on the proportions of roman Inscriptional letterforms.

Terminal
Strong and apparent influence of calligraphic nuances.

Axis
Axis of curved strokes is vertical.

For example, Metro (William Addison Dwiggins, 1880–1956), designed in 1929, which many identify as a Geometric, has a more apparent visual relationship with Gill Sans due to its varied-angled terminals.

Goudy Sans (Frederic Goudy, 1930) is a Humanist typeface that reflects Goudy's affinity for the traditions of Roman letterforms and manuscript lettering. Goudy Sans includes unorthodox elements for a Sans Serif Humanist such as a slight swelling of terminal strokes, select slab serifs, alternate uncials, a few swash strokes, and an italic.

Hermann Zapf's Optima (1958) can be classified as either a Humanist or a Glyphic. It reflects a strong calligraphic form with classic Roman proportions, as well as an obvious spread of slightly waisted strokes toward broadening terminals. Zapf describes

his renowned typeface as a "serifless roman" inspired by inscriptional lettering he had seen in Florence, Italy. It continues to be a popular typographic reference for calligraphers and stone carvers.

While Adrian Frutiger's Frutiger (1975) typeface was initially designed for the Charles de Gaulle Airport in Roissy, France, his overall design intent was to develop a Sans Serif Humanist typeface that possessed similar visual attributes to Univers (Adrian Frutiger, 1957, see pages 54, 137) paired with the humanistic characteristics of Gill Sans. His efforts produced one of the most functional sign system typefaces in terms of legibility used today.

Revival Sans Serif Humanist Typeface:

TheSans (1994)

Lucas de Groot (Dutch, b. 1963)

abcdefghijklmno

pqrstuvwxyz

ABCDEFGHIJKLM

NOPQRSTUVW

XYZ

0123456789

Type Designer Profile:

Lucas de Groot (Dutch, b. 1963)

Born in Noordwijkerhout, Netherlands, Luc(as) de Groot is a Berlin-based, Dutch type designer, graphic designer, educator, and head of the type foundries FontFabrik and LucasFonts. He is widely known for the popular and large font family, Thesis (TheSans, TheSerif, TheMix, TheSansMono, and TheAntiqua; 1994; see right) and Corpid (also known as AgroSans; 1997).

He also has designed custom fonts for international publications and newspapers such as *Folha de S. Paulo* (Brazil), *Le Monde* (France), *Der Spiegel* (Germany), and *Metro*, (the international free newspaper), as well as for international corporations including Sun Microsystems, Bell South, Heineken, Siemens, and Miele. De Groot designed two font families for Microsoft: the monospaced font family Consolas (2004), a new alternative to Courier, and Calibri (2004), a new default typeface for Microsoft Word.

In addition, de Groot is a member of the design faculty of the University of Applied Sciences in Potsdam, Germany.

Image: LucasFonts ©1994.

Visual Characteristics

Sans Serif Humanist typefaces reflect many of the same visual characteristics and proportions as serif typefaces due to their strong calligraphic influence. Their proportions are often derived from Roman inscriptional lettering and early serif typefaces.

Contrast in letterform stroke weight is apparent, with some featuring angled stress in comparison to most Sans Serifs, which consistently have a vertical axis. Many Sans Serif Humanist typefaces have a lowercase double-story "a" and lowercase single-story

"g." Due to their smaller x-height, legibility and readability of continuous text settings will be further enhanced with generous leading.

It is due to these visual characteristics that Humanist typefaces are the most legible and the most easily read of all of the Sans Serif typefaces.

Applications

Sans Serif Humanist typefaces function extremely well for settings of continuous text; however, they traditionally need to be set at a larger size due to their smaller x-height in comparison to the majority of Sans Serif Grotesque typefaces. They are also extremely compatible with classic Serif typefaces from Humanist (see page 17), Old Style (see page 23), and Transitional (see page 31) classifications since all have Roman letter proportions.

Contemporary Influence:

Unit

Unit (2003) is characteristically a twenty-first century Sans Serif Humanist typeface family designed by type designer Christian Schwartz (American, b. 1977) and type designer Erik Spiekermann (German, b. 1947). It is comprised of an extensive range of 14 weights, ranging from Thin to Ultra, including italics, and is ideally suited to a wide range of applications including branding, digital media, environmental graphics, packaging, and print media (see right).

Unit also provides advanced typographical support with features such as ligatures, small capitals, alternate characters, case-sensitive forms, fractions, and super- and subscript characters. Additionally, it comes with a complete range of figure set options—old style and lining figures, each in tabular and proportional widths—as well as supporting Cyrillic and Greek writing systems. In 2004, Unit received the distinguished Type Directors Club 2 award for typographic design excellence.

Reflecting the influence of Edward Johnston, Eric Gill (see page 64), William Addison Dwiggins, Frederic Goudy (see page 83), Hermann Zapf (see page 79), and Adrian Frutiger, Unit is a classic typeface in the Sans Serif Humanist typeface tradition and a definitive twenty-first-century design, making full use of the capabilities of diverse media.

Image: FontFont ©2010.

Since most Humanist typefaces are derived from the conventions of inscriptional lettering, they work extremely well in large-scale but are equally effective in book-scale text settings.

Seminal Sans Serif Humanist Typefaces:
Calibri (Lucas de Groot, 2004)
Frutiger (Adrian Frutiger, 1976)
Goudy Sans (Frederic Goudy, 1925)
Meta (Erik Spiekermann, 1986)
Myriad (Robert Slimbach,
    Carol Twombly, 1990)
Optima (Hermann Zapf, 1958)
Syntax (Hans Eduard Meier, 1972)
Trebuchet (Vincent Connare, 1996)
Unit (Christian Schwartz,
    Erik Spiekermann, 2003)
¶

Core Glyphic Typeface:
Albertus (1940)
Berthold Wolpe (German, 1905–1989)

abcdefghijklmnopq

rstuvwxyz

ABCDEFGHIJKLM

NOPQRSTUVW

XYZ

0123456789

Type Designer Profile:

Berthold Wolpe

(German, 1905–1989)

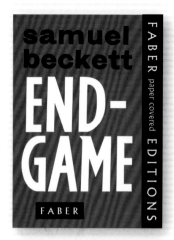

Berthold Wolpe was a German calligrapher, type designer, book designer, and illustrator. He began his professional career as an apprentice in a metalworking shop before studying with Rudolf Koch (German, 1876–1934) at the Offenbach Kunstgewerbeschule.

In 1935, he emigrated to England and began designing a typeface for type designer Stanley Morison (British, 1889–1967) and Monotype Corporation. The typeface, called Albertus, was introduced in 1940. In 1941, he joined the production department at Faber and Faber, a renowned British publisher, where he incorporated Albertus and many of his other hand-painted lettering in Faber paperback editions (see right). He remained at Faber until his retirement in 1975, where it is estimated that he designed over 1,500 book jackets and covers.

A retrospective exhibition of his work was held at the Victoria & Albert Museum (V&A) in 1980 and in Mainz, Germany in 2006. He was made a Royal Designer for Industry in 1959, awarded an honorary doctorate degree by the Royal College of Art in 1968, and appointed an Officer of the Order of the British Empire (OBE) in 1983.

Image: Faber & Faber Ltd. ©1958.

Glyphic

This type classification solely concerns itself with carved and inscribed typefaces that have their origins in the proportions and forms of classical Roman inscriptional lettering. The primary visual characteristic of Glyphic letterforms is that their stem or stroke broadens towards its terminal, sometimes identified as a vestigal serif or waisted stem.

A prime example of this classification is Albertus (Berthold Wolpe, 1940), a Glyphic typeface influenced by his earlier training as a lettering artist and calligrapher and by the German and Eastern European traditions of glyphic lettering.

While some Glyphic typefaces reference the traditions of Blackletter (see page 85), such as Neuland (Rudolf Koch, 1923), the majority of Glyphic typefaces are derived from traditional Roman letter proportions and profiles. This is clearly evident in Rusticana (Adrian Frutiger, 1992) and Lithos (Carol Twombly, 1990; see page 73) both of which are based on early Mediterranean inscriptional and ceremonial lettering.

Other faithful interpretations of classical inscriptional lettering include Trajan (1990; see page 72), Carol Twombly's visual interpretation of Roman lettering found on the Trajan column, one of the most popular Glyphic typefaces available today. Poppl Laudatio (Frederich Poppl, 1982) has a tall x-height and generous open counters that

Visual Characteristics:

Glyphic

Stroke
Minimum contrast in stroke weight.

Letterform
Chiseled forms with waisted stems

Terminal
Sharp, triangular-shaped serifs with angular terminals.

Axis (Or Stress)
Vertical axis of curved strokes.

make it more functional and appropriate for smaller text settings than most typefaces found in this type classification. Matthew Carter's Mantinia (1993; see page 56), based on inscriptional lettering found in Italian painter Andrea Mantegna's *The Entombment* (ca. 1470), includes an extensive and beautiful range of alternates, ligatures, superiors, and tall caps.

Visual Characteristics

While Glyphic typefaces could be classified as serifs, they are derived solely from engraved, carved, or chiseled letterforms. Glyphics, also known as "incised" typefaces, are sometimes limited to capital letterforms, with minimal serifs mirroring the hand-chiseled process.

Their visual characteristics include minimal contrast in stroke widths and a

vertical stress axis for most curved stroke letterforms. A distinctive visual detail on most Glyphic typefaces is a triangular-shaped serif or sharp, flared terminal located at the end of character strokes.

Applications

Glyphics are primarily used for titling and display purposes since the majority of these typefaces do not offer lowercase letterforms. For example, Mantinia (Matthew Carter, 1993; see page 56) and Trajan (Carol Twombly, 1990; see page 72) exist only in capital letterforms.

Some Glyphic typefaces can be effectively used for limited amounts of small-scale text settings, but careful consideration and visual analysis should be given before using any of these typefaces in this context.

Revival Glyphic Typeface:
Trajan (1990)
Carol Twombly (American, b. 1959)

ABCDEFGHIJKL MNOPQRSTUV WXYZ 0123456789

Seminal Glyphic Typefaces:
Augustea (Aldo Novarese,
    Alessandro Butti, 1951)
Charlemagne (Carol Twombly, 1989)
Fritz Quadrata (Ernst Friz,
    Victor Caruso, 1975)
Laudatio (Friedrich Poppl, 1982)
Lithos (Carol Twombly, 1990)
Mantinia (Matthew Carter, 1993)
Neuland (Rudolf Koch, 1923)
Rusticana (Adrian Frutiger, 1992)
¶

Carol Twombly

(American, b. 1959)

Myriad
TRAJAN
Chaparral Pro
Nueva
ROSEWOOD

Carol Twombly studied graphic design and architecture at the Rhode Island School of Design, where she first became interested in letterforms and type design. She subsequently received a master's degree from Stanford University in the digital typography graduate department under type designer Charles Bigelow (American, b. 1945) and later joined his firm, Bigelow & Holmes.

In 1984, Twombly won first prize from the Morisawa Typeface Design Competition for her Latin typeface Mirarae, which Bitstream subsequently produced. From 1988 to 1999, she worked as a staff designer at Adobe Systems, developing some of the most widely recognized digital fonts (see above) of the twentieth century, including Lithos (1990), based on inscribed Greek lettering; Trajan (1990), based on Roman capital letters found on the Trajan column; and Nueva (1994), Rosewood (1994), Chaparral Pro (2000), and Myriad (1992), designed with fellow Adobe Systems designer Robert Slimbach (American, b. 1956).

Twombly retired from Adobe in 1999 to pursue other design interests including jewelry and textile design.

Lithos

The earliest known sans-serif letterforms were carved Greek Ionic building inscriptions (see below), dating back to as early as the fifth century BCE. These were later used as inspiration for twentieth century type designers such as Carol Twombly (American, b. 1959) for her Sans Serif Glyphic typeface Lithos (1990).

The letterforms of this Glyphic typeface were derived from the Phoenician alphabet, which the Greeks modified into a system of twenty-five characters. It included five vowels (a, e, i, o, and u) and read from left to right; however, at this time there were still no visual separations between words and sentences, nor was there any punctuation. The Greek Ionic alphabet was the sole source of all modern European scripts and is considered the world's first true alphabet.

Image: ©British Museum.

Core Script Typeface:
Küenstler Script (1957)
Hans Bohn (German, 1891–1980)

abcdefghijklmnop

qrstuvwxyz

ABCDEFGHI

JKLMNOPQ

RSTUVWXYZ

0123456789

Type Designer Profile:

Hans Bohn

(German, 1891–1980)

Hans Bohn was born in 1891 in Oberlahn-stein, Germany. Following his education and training at the Technische Lehranstalt in Offenbach, Bohn began his professional career in 1914 at the Ullstein Verlag in Berlin. From 1919 to 1930, he worked as a type designer at the Klingspor Type Foundry and subsequently designed type-faces for the Ludwig & Mayer Type Foundry.

Following the Second World War, Bohn worked as a graphic and type designer for numerous German publishers, including Rowohlt, Schneekluth, Ullstein, and Fischer, as well as teaching graphic design at the Meisterschule für das gestaltende Handwerk (Offenbach).

In 1957, he designed Küenstler Script for the D. Stempel AG Foundry.

Script

The Script type classification is organized in three subcategories, namely Formal, Casual, and Calligraphic.

While the first known script or cursive letterforms (identified as "lettre courante" in France and "secretary hand" in England) originated as a formal genre of handwrit-ing and were cut by Robert Granjon (French, 1513–1589) in the mid-sixteenth century, the first script-based typefaces, identified as Chancery, were produced in Italy at the end of the fifteenth century. Twentieth-century Chancery-like script typefaces include Zapf Chancery (Hermann Zapf, 1979), as well as Poetica (Robert Slimbach, 1992)—an extensive script type family including a wide range of alternate characters, ornaments, and swashes.

Formal Script typefaces derive from seventeenth-century handwriting genres with many having slanted, rounded characters with flowing strokes that often connect them to other letterforms. These scripts include an extensive range of typefaces from the very formal Snell Roundhand (Matthew Carter, 1966) to the casual Ashley Script (Ashley Havinden, 1955).

Casual Script typefaces have an informal or hand-drawn appearance, such as with a pen or brush. Letterform strokes typically connect one letter to the next. These typefaces cover a range of graphic representations from the informal Brush Script (Robert E. Smith, 1942) to the spontaneous Pronto (Alejandro Paul, 2009).

Calligraphic Script typefaces derive from calligraphic handwriting, and their letterforms can either be connected or non-connected, with many appearing as if written with a flat-nibbed writing tool. These typefaces include a diverse range of visual representa-tions from the refined Vivaldi (Fritz Peters, 1990) to the expressive Riptide (Timothy Donaldson, 1996).

Adios Script (2012)

Alejandro Paul (Argentinean, b. 1972)

abcdefghijklmnopqrs

tuvwxyz

ABCDEFGHI

JKLMNOPQ

RSTUVWXYZ

0123456789

Type Designer Profile:
Alejandro Paul
(Argentinean, b. 1972)

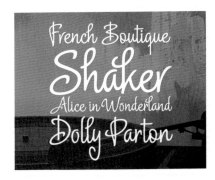

Alejandro Paul is one of the founders of the Sudtipos project, the first Argentine type foundry collective (whose other members include Ariel Garofalo, Claudio Pousada, and Diego Giaccone).

Paul taught graphic design and typography at the Universidad de Buenos Aires from 1996 until 2004, and has worked as an art director in Argentine studios handling corporate brands such as Arcor, Proctor & Gamble, SC Johnson, Danone, and others.

In 2003, he began designing fonts and lettering for several packaging agencies, creating some of his best-known work to date including the typeface Delight Script (with Angel Koziupa, 2011; see above). In 2006, he presented at TMDG06, the largest Latin American graphic design event, attended by more than 4,000 designers, and he has been invited to speak at design and typography conferences in Portugal, Germany, Chile, Brazil, Ecuador, Uruguay, Mexico, Canada, and the United States. His work has been featured in *STEP Inside Design, Creative Review, Print, Computer Arts, Visual, Creative Arts,* and *Novum.* In 2009, Paul received his second Type Directors Club award for his typeface Adios Script (2009).

Image: Sudtipos ©2011.

Visual Characteristics
All Script typefaces in this type classification share one universal visual characteristic—they all appear to have been written by hand rather than cast, sculpted, or mechanically drawn.

They also possess a wide diversity of visual styles and nuances including formal, informal, upright, or cursive; display strong contrasts in thick and thin strokes; have angled letterforms with high ascenders and deep descenders; and connect with each other or stand separate and apart from one another.

Applications
The primary function of Script typefaces is decorative since few, if any, are appropriate for text-scale settings or extended passages of running text. They are traditionally used for titling or display purposes.

Seminal Script Typefaces:
Bickham Script (Richard Lipton, 1997)
Byron (Pat Hickson, 1992)
Cascade (Matthew Carter, 1966)
Choc (Roger Excoffon, 1955)
Citadel (Monotype Design Studio, 2003)
Coronet (Robert Hunter Middleton, 1937)
Isadora (Kris Holmes, 1985)
Monoline Script (Monotype Design Studio, 1933)
Riptide (Timothy Donaldson, 1996)
Snell Roundhand (Matthew Carter, 1966)
Vivaldi (Fritz Peters, 1970)
Zapf Chancery (Hermann Zapf, 1979)
¶

Core Decorative Typeface:

Saphir (1953)

Hermann Zapf (German, 1918–2015)

ABCDEFGHI
JKLMNOPQ
RSTUVWXYZ
123456789

Decorative

The typefaces within the Decorative type classification stem from wood-engraved initial caps found in printed books of the fifteenth and sixteenth centuries. The first known Decorative typeface was Union Pearl (ca. 1690), attributed to the Grover Type Foundry in England.

In the eighteenth century, numerous Decorative typefaces were developed by English and French type foundries to meet the new demand for advertisements, broadsides, and posters. As the need for greater differentiation of products and services grew throughout the late nineteenth and early twentieth centuries, an abundance of varied Decorative typefaces with a diverse range of visual characteristics continued to be introduced.

Decorative typefaces are also known as Ornamental, Specialty, or Novelty.

Type Designer Profile:

Hermann Zapf

(German, 1918–2015)

Herman Zapf was born in Nuremberg, Germany in 1918 and was a master calligrapher, artist, and educator, and one of the most prolific type designers of the twentieth century. He created more than 175 typefaces for metal type foundries, photo compositors, and digital foundries. Two of his most renowned typefaces are Palatino (1950), Renaissance Antiqua (1984; see right) and Optima (1958). The latter, which he called a "serif-less Roman," was inspired by inscriptional lettering he had seen in Florence and still remains extremely popular with calligraphers and stone carvers.

A self-taught type and book designer since 1938, Zapf worked for D. Stempel AG, Mergenthaler Linotype Company, Berthold, Hell Digiset, Hallmark Cards, and International Typeface Corporation. In 1977, he became a professor of typographic computer programming at the Rochester Institute of Technology in New York State.

Zapf received numerous awards for his typographic work including the 1989 Gold Medal at the International Buchkunst-Austellung in Leipzig, the Frederic W. Goudy Award in Typography from Rochester Institute of Technology in 1969, and the Gutenberg Prize for technical and aesthetic achievement in type in 1974. He was also made an Honorary Royal Designer for Industry in London in 1989.

In 2010, Zapf was awarded the Order of Merit of the Federal Republic of Germany.

Image: Cary Graphic Arts Collection, Rochester Institute of Technology.

Visual Characteristics

All typefaces in this type classification share one universal visual characteristic—they all were designed for limited use at larger display sizes rather than for smaller-scale, continuous text settings. Many possess added ornaments, internal decoration, and inlines or outlines to their letterforms.

Applications

The Decorative type classification includes a wide stylistic array of display typefaces that were developed for limited use at large sizes, rather than for text settings. These display typefaces include versions with stencils, outlines, shadows, inlines, decorative ornamentation, flourishes, dimensionality, and distortion, as well as display typefaces that mimic a wide range of historical visual

Revival Decorative Typeface:
Arcadia (1990)
Neville Brody (British, b. 1957)

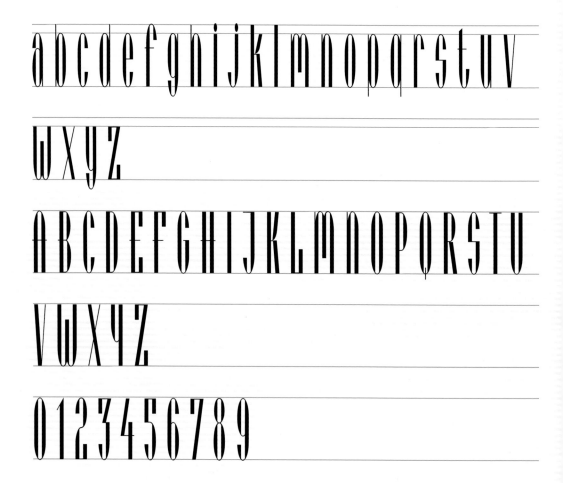

Type Designer Profile:
Neville Brody
(British, b. 1957)

Renowned British graphic designer, art director, typographer, and educator Neville Brody gained public acclaim in the early 1980s with his highly innovative approach to typography.

He was born in London in 1957 and attended the London College of Printing and Hornsey College of Art. His early work included experimental and revolutionary combinations of typographic expression for magazines such as *The Face* (see right) and *Arena*, as well as for independent music labels and artists such as Cabaret Voltaire and Depeche Mode.

In 1988, the first of two volumes about his work—*The Graphic Language of Neville Brody*—became the world's first best-selling book on graphic design, and an accompanying exhibition on his graphic design work and typography at the Victoria and Albert Museum (V&A) drew more than 40,000 visitors before it traveled to Europe and Japan. In 1991, Brody started the design consultancy Research Studios, the type foundry Fontworks, and *Fuse*, a regularly published collection of experimental typefaces continually challenging the boundaries of editorial, graphic, and type design.

In 2011, Brody was named the new head of the Communication Art and Design Department at London's Royal College of Art.

Image: Bauer Media ©1990.

styles ranging from Art Nouveau and Art Deco to Modernism, Post-Modernism, pop culture, and the digital age.

Seminal Decorative Typefaces:
Broadway (Morris Fuller Benton, 1929)
Copperplate (Frederic Goudy, 1901)
Eckmann (Otto Eckmann, 1900)
Empire (Morris Fuller Benton, 1927)
Entropy (Stephen Farrell, 1993)
Ironmonger (John Downer, 1991)
Neuland (Rudolf Koch, 1923)
Peignot (A. M. Cassandre, 1937)
Umbra (Robert Hunter Middleton, 1932)
Sophia (Matthew Carter, 1993)
Umbra (Robert Hunter Middleton, 1932)
Zombie (Christian Schwartz, 1993)
¶

Core Blackletter Typeface:
Goudy Text (1928)
Frederic Goudy (American, 1865–1947)

abcdefghijklmnopqrst

vwxyz

ABCDEFGHIJ

KLMNOPQRS

TUVWXYZ

0123456789

Type Designer Profile:
Frederic Goudy
(American, 1865–1947)

Frederic Goudy was one of the most prolific American type designers of the twentieth century. By his own account, he designed 123 faces (though he counted each italic as a separate typeface).

Goudy, born in Bloomington, Illinois in 1865, was interested in type at an early age. He held several jobs in various cities before founding a printing business, the Booklet Press, in Chicago in 1895. Renamed the Camelot Press, he printed the journal *American Cap-Book* before selling his interest a year later.

In his next successful endeavor, he sold a set of capital letterforms of his own design to the Bruce Type Foundry in Boston, which encouraged him to become a freelance lettering artist. He also taught lettering and graphic design at the Frank Holme School of Illustration. In 1903, Goudy started The Village Press in partnership with graphic designer Will Ransom (American, 1878–1955) in Park Ridge, Illinois.

Goudy's breakthrough came in 1911 when he designed Kennerley Old Style. Subsequently, he set up the Village Letter Foundry to cast and sell Kennerley and a titling font, Forum (1912), which established his reputation as a type designer. American Type Founders (ATF) commissioned Goudy to design a typeface, resulting in Goudy Old Style (1915), regarded by many critics as one of his finest typefaces. In 1920, with forty typefaces to his name, Goudy became Lanston Monotype's appointed art adviser.

As one of his final influences, Goudy wrote about type and the origins of his work in his book *A Half Century of Type Design and Typography: 1895-1945* (1946; see above), completed when he was nearly eighty years old.

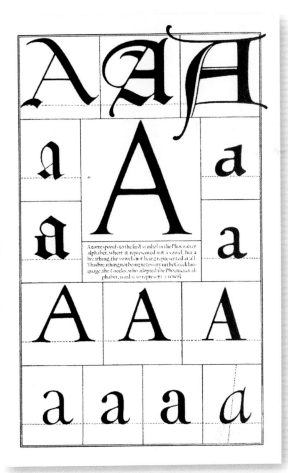

Revival Blackletter Typeface:
Bastard (1990)
Jonathan Barnbrook (British, b. 1966)

Type Designer Profile:
Jonathan Barnbrook
(British, b. 1966)

Jonathan Barnbrook is a British typographer and graphic designer. Born in Luton in 1966, Barnbrook studied at Central Saint Martins College of Art & Design from 1985 to 1988 and at the Royal College of Art from 1988 to 1990.

Initial recognition for his typographic work came for his cover art for David Bowie's 2002 album *Heathen*, which featured the debut of Barnbrook's Priori (2003) typeface. Barnbrook has worked with London's why not associates, and in 1990 started freelancing as a graphic designer. In 1996, he launched his own digital type foundry, Virus.

Other well-known typefaces designed by Barnbrook, such as Exocet (1990), False Idol (1997), Infidel (2004; see above), and Mason (1991), have emotional and controversial titles reflecting the style and themes found in most of his work.

Image: Jonathan Barnbrook ©2004.

Blackletter

Blackletter, also known as Gothic Script or Gothic Minuscule, was developed as a formal Latin script-based type genre or minuscule (see page 21) and used primarily throughout Western Europe from the late-twelfth century to the seventeenth century.

Early typographic forms of Blackletter were introduced by Johannes Gutenberg (German, 1398–1468), the inventor of movable metal type, in the mid-fifteenth century. His iconic *42-Line Bible* (ca. 1455; see page 86) was the first book to utilize this new printing technology as well as metal type mimicking a dense textura cursive script traditionally hand-lettered by German scribes of the day.

The Blackletter type classification is organized in four separate and distinct subcategories, namely Textura, Bastarda (or Schwabacher), Fraktur, and Rotunda.

Contemporary interpretations of these subcategories include Totally Gothic (Zuzana Licko, 1990), Licko's interpretation of a Blackletter Textura originally autotraced in Fontographer with curvilinear letterforms reflecting both calligraphic and digital bitmapped profiles; and Bastard (Jonathan Barnbrook, 1990), Barnbrook's exploration of a Blackletter digital typeface based on a monastic script with angular terminals but drawn electronically avoiding curvilinear letter strokes and profiles. It is available in three weights, namely Spindly Bastard, Fat Bastard, and Even Fatter Bastard.

Visual Characteristics

Blackletter typefaces are characterized by pointed and angular forms, and high contrast between thick and thin strokes, and are modeled on late medieval manuscript lettering drawn with a broad-nibbed pen.

Textura is an early Blackletter type used in the Gutenberg Bible (ca. 1455) and has a closed set of vertical letterforms with hexagonal lowercase letters, angled ascenders and descenders, with angular, pointed forms, where their stroke weight and width exceeds the white space of both counters and inter-character spacing.

Bastarda references the Carolingian Minuscule (see page 21) and derives from the Humanist influence of Italian type design in the fifteenth century. It is characterized by slightly condensed lowercase letters, angled ascenders and descenders, and pointed forms. It is highly legible and was the most commonly used Blackletter typeface in Germany until it was replaced by Fraktur in the mid-sixteenth century.

Fraktur derives from the Chancery genre of the late-fifteenth and early sixteenth centuries and is characterized by D-shaped lowercase letters, broken curves, dramatic and exaggerated curved strokes, swashed terminals, and curved tails.

Rotunda is a highly legible version of Blackletter with circular lowercase letters, thick terminals, straight stems and downstrokes, and an angled stress evident in rounded letterforms.

Applications

While Blackletter for dense book-scale text settings was replaced in the late-fifteenth century by Humanist (see page 17) serif typefaces throughout Western Europe, it still remains a relevant typeface choice for select contemporary applications.

In most contemporary applications, it is traditionally considered as a display-style typeface adapted for religious or political contexts, as well as to communicate a sense of the past. When combining any style of Blackletter with other roman typefaces, the designer should take into consideration its weight and color in relationship to the typeface that it is paired with, making sure that it is equally strong so that it is not visually overpowered or lost in its final application.

Seminal Blackletter Typefaces:

Cloister Black (Morris Fuller Benton, 1904)

Duc De Berry (Gottfried Pott, 1990)

Fette Fraktur (C. E. Weber, 1875)

Klingspor Gotisch (Rudolf Koch, 1925)

Libra (Sjoerd Hendrik de Roos, 1938)

Ondine (Adrian Frutiger, 1954)

Totally Gothic (Zuzana Licko, 1990)

Uncial (Victor Hammer, 1952)

¶

page from 42-line Bible ca. 1455
Johannes Gutenberg
(German, 1398–1468)

Image: Lilly Library, Indiana University, Bloomington, Indiana.

A page from the Gutenberg Bible, the first book printed with movable type, shows an early version of Textura Blackletter.

Test your Knowledge

1. What type classification marks the start of the refinement of typographic form from centuries of handwritten and calligraphic-based letterforms to a more articulated and delineated type genre?

2. The term Garalde is another identifier for what type classification?

3. What type classification includes the typefaces Bembo, Garamond, and Goudy?

4. Identify the primary visual characteristics of Transitional typefaces.

5. Which of the following fonts are not identified as Transitional typefaces: (a) Bembo (b) Bodoni (c) Caledonia (d) Melior (e) Sabon (f) Times New Roman?

6. What type classification was highly influenced by the typefaces designed by Giambattista Bodoni and Firmin Didot?

7. Identify the primary visual characteristics of Modern typefaces.

8. What type classification is used to identify the first display typefaces specifically designed for large-scale display needs?

9. What are the four (4) subcategories of the Sans Serif type classification?

10. Identify the primary visual characteristics of Glyphic typefaces.

11. What term is used to identify the first script-based typefaces that were produced in Italy at the end of the fifteenth century?

12. What are the three (3) subcategories of the Script type classification?

13. What is the type classification that includes ornamental, specialty, and novelty typefaces?

14. What are the four (4) separate and distinct subcategories of the Blackletter type classification?

For answers to Test your Knowledge, see page 228.

Section 2

Terminology

T he foundation of any successful graphic designer depends upon their understanding of the fundamental elements of type, a crucially important skill which underpins almost every other aspect of type. This section provides an in-depth understanding of the anatomical elements and terminology of type—what they are, why they are important, how to identify them, and how to use them effectively.

    To better understand, appreciate, and recognize the multitude of anatomical terms applicable to type, as well as the similarities and differences between

Type Anatomy

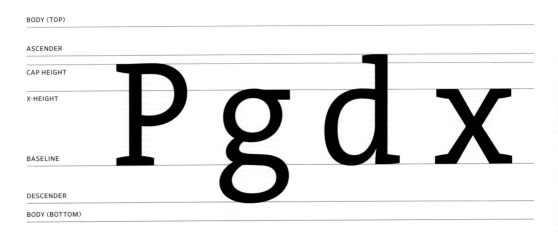

typefaces, a well-rounded and informed graphic designer needs to be familiar with the form, structure, and anatomy of letterforms. Each typeface has a very distinct and unique appearance, as well as characteristics and features that provide distinguishing details to group together or set typefaces apart from one another. This essential understanding will ultimately affect your visual judgments and facilitate better and more meaningful decisions in making selections and applications with any typeface.

The terminology of type is also an essential reference tool for any graphic designer to understand and be familiar with, since it provides a universal language to describe the various parts of letterforms as well as the ability to analyze and compare their individual characteristics.

7 n

Alternate Character
An additional letterform different in graphic form than its standard design. An example is *lining figures* in comparison to *old style (non-lining) figures*.

Aperture
The rounded, partially enclosed negative space in a letterform such as an n, C, S, and the lower part of an e or the upper story of an a.

Apex
The outer point where two diagonal stems or strokes meet. Apex points can be either pointed, rounded, flat, or extended.

f E d

Arc
A curved stroke that extends from a straight stem of a letterform but does not form a bowl; such as the top or bottom of a lowercase f.

Arm
A projecting horizontal or upward diagonal stem or stroke of a letterform not enclosed within a character, as in an E, K, or L.

Ascender
The part of a lowercase letterform that extends above the body of the letterform, or x-height, as in a b, d, f, h, l, and t.

G   d   I

Beard
A spur located at the bottom of a chin on some capital Gs.

HELVETICA (1956)

Bowl
A curved stem or stroke of a letterform that encloses a counter, as in a lowercase b, p, or O.

Bracket
A continuous, curving joint connecting a serif to a stem or stroke of a letterform. Also called *fillet*.

W   y   i

Crotch
The point where two strokes or stems of a letterform meet at an angle, as in a k, v, and w.

Descender
The part of a lowercase letterform that falls below the body of the letterform or baseline, as in a g, j, p, q, and y.

Dot
A punctuation glyph in the form of a typographic dot that either is used at the end of a sentence or caps the strokes of a lowercase i and j.

G p H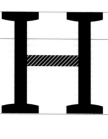

Chin
A stemmed stroke located at the bottom right of a capital G. Also called *jaw* or *hook*.

Counter
An area fully or partially enclosed by a bowl or a cross bar of a letterform, as in a b, p, o, or A.

Cross Bar
A horizontal element of a letterform connecting two vertical or diagonal stems or strokes, or crossing a stem or a stroke, as in an A, H, f, or t. Also called *bar* or *cross stroke*.

a g 5

Double-Story
A lowercase g with a closed, top counter connected by a link stroke to a looped tail, or a lowercase upright finial a.

Ear
A small projecting stroke sometimes attached to the bowl of a lowercase g or the stem of a lowercase r.

Flag
A horizontal stroke on the numeral 5.

Type Anatomy continued

x Y R

Foot
The base of a letterform,
which normally sits on
a baseline.

Fork
The intersection point
within a letterform
where one stroke splits
into two strokes as in a Y.

Joint
The angle formed in
a letterform where two
strokes meet or
intersect, as in a K or R.

g T o

Loop
The counter or
descender of a lower-
case, double-story g
when it is entirely
enclosed.

Overhang
An ascender of a
letterform that extends
into the space of a
previous or subsequent
character as with f, *f*, F,
T, and V.

Overshoot
The rounded or pointed
feature of a letterform
which extends slightly
over a baseline, x-height,
or cap line to optically
align with another
letterform that has
straight features. This
extension occurs with A,
a, C, c, d, e, G, g, m, n, O, o,
P, p, Q, q, r, S, s, U, u, V, v,
W, w, and V.

K

Leg
A projecting diagonal stem or stroke of a letterform extending downward, as in an R and K. Also called *tail*.

fi

Ligature
A stem or stroke that connects two or more letterforms together that form a ligature, tied letterform, or single glyph, as in fi and fl.

g

Link
A stem or stroke of a letterform that connects the bowl and the loop of a g.

F

Serif
The beginning or end of a stem or stroke, arm, leg, or tail drawn at a right angle or at an oblique angle to the stem or stroke of a letterform.

n

Shoulder
The portion of a curved stroke projecting from a stem of a letterform, but not the hairline, connecting two vertical strokes or stems.

g

Single-Story
A lowercase a with a closed bowl without a finial arm located above, or a lowercase g with a closed bowl, stem, and tail.

Type Anatomy continued

S G V

Spine
The diagonal portion or
main curved stroke of
an S or s.

Spur
A small, pointed
projection found at the
end of a stem or stroke
of a letterform,
sometimes located on
the bottom of a b, t, or G.
BASKERVILLE (1757)

Stem (or Stroke)
The principal vertical or
oblique element(s) of
a letterform, as in an A,
B, L, or V; except for a
curved letterform,
where it is called stroke.

Q

Tail
The short stem or stroke
of a letterform that rests
on a baseline, as in a K or
R, or extending below a
baseline, as in a Q or j. In
K and R. Also called *leg*.

Terminal (or Finial)
The end of any stem or
stroke of a letterform
that does not terminate
with a serif. See also
sheared terminal.

**Tie (or Connecting
Stroke)**
A stroke that joins two
letterforms together
to create a ligature (or
tied letterform).

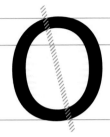

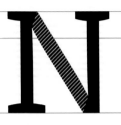

Stress (or Axis)
The inclination of thin and thick, curved stems or strokes (vertical or oblique) in a letterform, which can be an inclined or vertical stress or axis.

Stroke
The main diagonal component of a letterform, as in an N or Y.

Swash
A flourished terminal, stem, or stroke added to a letterform.

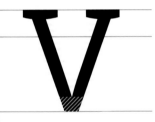

Vertex
The lower point of a letterform where stems of a character meet to form a junction with an angle of less than ninety degrees, for example, at the base of a capital or uppercase V.

Serif Anatomy

Abrupt Serif
An angled connection between a stem and a serif. Also called *unbracketed serif*.
THESERIF (1994)

Adnate Serif
A continuous and curved connection between a stem and a serif. Also called *bracketed serif* or *fillet serif*.
BASKERVILLE (1757)

Bifurcated Serif
A serif formed from a main stroke terminating in one or more splits.
MR. DARCY (2014)

Fillet Serif
see Adnate Serif.
GARAMOND (CA. 1530)

Hairline Serif
The thinnest of serif forms as found in Modern typefaces.
DIDOT (1799)

Rounded Serif
A serif with a rounded form.
JENSON (1471)

Unilateral Serif
A serif extending to one side of its main stroke.
THESERIF (1994)

Wedge Serif
A triangular form of serif.
ALBERTUS (1940)

Bilateral Serif

**A serif extending
to either side of its
main stroke.**

MRS. EAVES (1998)

Bracketed Serif

see Adnate Serif.

CLARENDON (1845)

Cupped Serif

**A serif with a cupped
bracket.**

JENSON (1471)

Scutulate

**A terminated stroke
that is diamond-shaped;
usually found in
Blackletter serifs.**

GOUDY TEXT (1928)

Slab Serif

**A large, broad serif
with a squared end,
either bracketed
or unbracketed.**

ARCHER (2001)

Unbracketed Serif

**A serif that connects
with the stem of a letterform at a ninety-degree
angle, such as in Didot.**

DIDOT (1799)

Terminal Anatomy

t   t   c

Acute Terminal
**A terminating stroke
that thins at its end
without a serif. Also
called *tapered terminal*.**
JENSON (1471)

Angled Terminal
**A terminating stroke cut
at an angle.**
THESERIF (1994)

Ball Terminal
**A circular terminal
located at the end of an
arm, as in a lowercase
a, c, or r.**
BODONI (1798)

k   a   t

Flared Terminal
**A terminating stroke
that widens at its end
without a serif.**
ALBERTUS (1940)

Hooked Terminal
**A terminating stroke
that is hooked at its end
without a serif.**
CLARENDON (1845)

Horizontal Terminal
**A terminating stroke
that is horizontally cut.**
FF DIN (1995)

f   n   k

Sheared Terminal
**An abrupt and almost
perpendicular
terminating stroke.**
THESANS (1994)

Squared Terminal
**A terminated stroke that
is squared at its end.**
CLARENDON (1845)

Straight Terminal
**A terminated stroke that
is cut perpendicular to
its main stroke.**
HELVETICA (1956)

r u x

Beak Terminal
A sharp terminal that appears at the end of the arc of a lowercase f, as well as in a c, j, r, and y.
CENTAUR (1914)

Concave Terminal
A concave termination of a stroke.
OPTIMA (1955)

Convex Terminal
A convex termination of a stroke.
GOTHAM ROUNDED (2005)

 j a t

Lachrymal Terminal
see Teardrop Terminal.
BASKERVILLE (1757)

Rounded Terminal
A terminating stroke that is rounded.
MRS. EAVES (1994)

Scalloped Terminal
A terminated stroke that is scalloped or scooped.
DIDOT (1799)

 t r z

Tapered Terminal
see Acute Terminal.
JENSON (1741)

Teardrop Terminal
A teardrop-shaped terminal located at a stroke end to a lowercase letterform such as f, j, and r in some typefaces. Also called *lachrymal terminal*.
SABON (1964)

Vertical Terminal
A terminating stroke that is vertically cut.
FUTURA (1927)

Key Typographic Terms

Type Classifications

Familiarity with the following terminology will provide you with a greater understanding and sensitivity to the visual harmony and complexity of type.

Calligraphic

Roman or italic typefaces based upon hand-rendered, script letterforms drawn with a flat-nibbed pen or brush. See also Uncial.

UNCIAL (1952)

Chancery

Chancery is the term used to identify script-based typefaces produced in Italy at the end of the fifteenth century.

ZAPF CHANCERY (1979)

Clarendon

A Slab Serif type classification characterized by strokes with even weight and heavy, bracketed serifs; Clarendon (Robert Besley, Benjamin Fox, 1845; see page 41) and Ionic (Chauncey Griffith, 1925) are seminal examples of Clarendon Slab Serif typefaces. Also called *Ionics*, *Mécanes*, or *Mechanicals*.

CLARENDON (1845)

Aldine

Typefaces, including roman, italic, and Greek, designed by Aldus Manutius (Italian, 1415–1550) and cut by Francesco Griffo (Italian, ca. 1450–1518) at the end of the fifteenth century.

ALDUS (1954)

Bastarda

A version of Blackletter characterized by slightly condensed lowercase letters, angled ascenders and descenders, and pointed forms.

DUC DE BERRY (1990)

Blackletter

A type classification based on early Germanic scribe-based letterforms that feature elaborate thick-to-thin straight strokes and serifs, narrow counter spacing, and tight leading, producing a heavy "black" color on the page. The Gutenberg Bible (ca. 1455), the first book to be printed with movable type, was set in a Blackletter typeface to mimic manuscript handwriting of the period. Variations of Blackletter include Textura, Bastarda, Fraktur, and Rotunda.

GOUDY TEXT (1928)

Cursive

See Script.

Decorative

A type classification that features highly stylized, one-of-a-kind typefaces that are primarily used for display titles or headlines. Also called *Novelty*, *Ornamental*, or *Specialty*.

SAPHIR (1953)

Didone

see Modern.

a Egyptian
A Slab Serif type classification characterized by traditional slab or square serifs and lacking in contrast to the thickness of its stems. Memphis (Emil Rudolf Weiss, 1929) and Rockwell (Frank Hinman Pierpont, 1934) are seminal examples of Egyptian slab serif typefaces. Also called *Ionics*, *Mécanes*, or *Mechanicals*.
ROCKWELL (1934)

Foundry
A commercial enterprise that designs, produces, and sells type.

u Fraktur
A version of Blackletter characterized by D-shaped lowercase letters, swashed terminals, and exaggerated, curved forms.
FETTE FRAKTUR (1875)

Garalde
see Old Style.

a Geometric
A Sans Serif type classification with characters that have minimal stroke contrast and are based on simple geometric shapes, such as circles, squares, and triangles. Futura (Paul Renner, 1927; see page 57) and Kabel (Rudolf Koch, 1927) are seminal examples of Geometric Sans Serif typefaces.
FUTURA (1927)

a Glyphic
A serif type classification that is derived solely from engraved, carved, or chiseled letterforms. Albertus (Berthold Wolpe, 1940; see page 69) and Trajan (Carol Twombly, 1990; see page 72) are seminal examples of Glyphic serif typefaces. Also called *Incised*.
ALBERTUS (1940)

a Gothic
A Sans Serif type classification with characters that have minimal contrast between stems and other strokes and no ornamentation. Gothic Sans Serif typefaces often contain the word as part of their name, as in Franklin Gothic (Morris Fuller Benton, 1903; see page 46), News Gothic (Morris Fuller Benton, 1908), and Trade Gothic (Jackson Burke, 1948).
NEWS GOTHIC (1908)

a Grotesque (Sans Serif)
A Sans Serif type classification with characters that lack serifs, have varying stroke contrast, a large x-height, and little or no stress in their rounded letterforms. Akzidenz Grotesk (1896) and Franklin Gothic (Morris Fuller Benton, 1903; see page 46) are seminal examples of Grotesque Sans Serif typefaces. Also called *Gothic* or *Grotesk*.
FRANKLIN GOTHIC (1903)

Hot-Metal
Type created from a mechanical composition system using molten lead casts in brass matrices.

a Humanist (Serif)
A serif type classification that is extremely calligraphic in appearance and possesses minimal contrast between thick and thin strokes, a small x-height, and a strong inclined stress reflecting earlier letterforms drawn with a broad-nibbed pen; also known as Venetian. Golden (William Morris, 1890) and Centaur (Bruce Rogers, 1914; see page 19) are seminal examples of Humanist serif typefaces.
CENTAUR (1914)

a

Humanist (Sans Serif)
A Sans Serif type classification based on the proportions of roman inscriptions. Gill Sans (Arthur Eric Rowton Gill, 1927; see page 63) and Frutiger (Adrian Frutiger, 1976) are seminal examples of Humanist Sans Serif typefaces.
GILL SANS (1927)

Ionic
see Clarendon.

Lineale
see Sans Serif.

Linotype
A mechanical typesetting system designed to cast whole lines or slugs of metal type. See also *mechanical composition*.

a

Modern
A serif type classification characterized by extreme contrast between thick and thin strokes, as well as flat serifs. Didot (Firmin Didot, 1799) and Bodoni (Giambattista Bodoni, 1798; see page 35) are seminal examples of Modern serif typefaces. Also called *Didone*.
DIDOT (1799)

a

Neo-Grotesque
A Sans Serif type classification with characters that have consistent stroke widths and contrast, closed apertures, circular forms, and horizontal terminals. Helvetica (Max Miedinger, 1956; see page 51) and Univers (Adrian Frutiger, 1976; see pages 54, 137) are seminal examples of Neo-Grotesque Sans Serif typefaces.
HELVETICA (1956)

Novelty
see Decorative.

Old English
see Blackletter.

a

Old Style
A serif type classification based on early roman typefaces, characterized by low contrast between thick and thin strokes, a left-leaning axis or stress, and bracketed serifs. Garamond (Claude Garamond, ca. 1530; see page 22) and Sabon (Jan Tschichold, 1964; see page 26) are seminal examples of Old Style serif typefaces. Also called *Garalde*.
GARAMOND (CA. 1530)

Ornamental
see Decorative.

Revival
An adaptation of an existing typeface for newer technologies or methods of printing or reproduction.

a

Rotunda
A version of Blackletter characterized by angular pointed forms; circular lower-case letterforms, and straight stems.
ONDINE (1954)

a

Sans Serif
A type classification that does not feature serifs (sans means "without" in French). There are four main categories within this type classification: Grotesque, Neo-Grotesque, Geometric, and Humanist. Also called *Lineale*.
HELVETICA (1956)

Script

A type classification characterized by handwritten letterforms that may be either formal or informal. The term Script, including Calligraphic, Casual, and Formal, usually denotes linked letterforms rather than unlinked cursive letterforms.

Formal script typefaces, reflecting seventeenth-century handwriting styles, are visually neat, regular, and flowing. Casual script typefaces, reflecting contemporary cursive and print handwriting styles, are often playful and unconventional in appearance. Calligraphic script typefaces reflect calligraphic handwriting styles and often appear written with a flat-nibbed pen or writing instrument. Also called *Cursive*. Snell Roundhand (Matthew Carter, 1966) and Zapf Chancery (Hermann Zapf, 1979) are seminal examples of Script typefaces.

KÜENSTLER SCRIPT (1902)

Serif/Sans Serif

Serifs are small strokes located at the end of a main vertical or horizontal stroke of a letterform that aid reading by helping to lead the eye across a line of text. Serif is also used as a classification for typefaces containing decorative, pointed, rounded, slab or square serif finishing strokes. Sans Serif fonts lack these decorative elements and typically have little stroke variation, larger x-heights, and no stress in rounded strokes.

Slab Serif

A serif type classification characterized by large, broad serifs with a squared end, either bracketed or unbracketed. Also called *Antique*, *Egyptian*, *Egyptienne*, or *Square Serif*. Memphis (Emil Rudolf Weiss, 1929) and Rockwell (Frank Hinman Pierpont, 1934) are seminal examples of Slab Serif typefaces.

ROCKWELL (1934)

Specialty

see Decorative.

Textura

A version of Blackletter characterized by hexagonal lowercase letterforms and angular, pointed forms.

GOUDY TEXT (1928)

Transitional

A serif type classification characterized by a subtle contrast between thick and thin strokes, minimal left-inclined stress, and a triangular or flat tip where diagonal strokes meet, such as at the base of a W. Caslon (William Caslon, 1725) and Baskerville (John Baskerville, 1757; see page 29) are seminal examples of Transitional serif typefaces.

BASKERVILLE (1757)

Uncial

A type style related to calligraphy, or a majuscule script, with rounded, unconnected letterforms that are evident in fourth to eighth century European manuscripts. Uncials are the basis for modern capital letterforms. See also Calligraphic.

UNCIAL (1952)

Key Typographic Terms continued

Type Anatomy

n

Aperture
The rounded, partially enclosed negative space in a letterform such as a n, C, S, and the lower part of an e or the upper story of an a. See also Counter.

A

Apex
The outer point of a letterform where two diagonal stems or strokes meet, as at the highest point of an A or M or at the bottom of an M. Apex points can be either pointed, rounded, flat, or extended.

f

Arc
A curved stroke of a letterform that extends from a straight stem but does not form a bowl; such as the top or bottom of a lowercase f.

k

Arm
A projecting horizontal or upward diagonal stem or stroke of a letterform not enclosed within a character, as in an E, K, or L.

b

Ascender
The part of a lowercase letterform that extends above the body of the letterform, or x-height, as in a b, d, f, h, l, and t.

Bar
see Cross Bar, Cross Stroke.

G

Beard
A spur located at the bottom of a chin on some capital Gs.

HELVETICA (1956)

O

Bowl
A curved stem or stroke of a letterform that encloses a counter, as in a lowercase b, p, or O. Also called *eye*.

I

Bracket
A continuous, curving joint of a letterform connecting a serif to a stem or stroke. Also called *fillet*.

CLARENDON (1845)

G

Chin
A stemmed stroke located at the bottom right of a capital G. Also called *jaw* or *hook*.

o

Counter
An area fully or partially enclosed by a bowl or a cross bar of a letterform, as in a b, p, o, or A. The counter is also called an eye for a lowercase e, and a loop for the bowl created in the descender of a lowercase g. A counter can also describe the shape of the negative space within an open letterform, for example an uppercase C. Also called *aperture*.

f

Cross Bar
A horizontal element connecting two vertical or diagonal stems or strokes of a letterform, or crossing a stem or a stroke of a letterform, as in an A, H, f, or t. Also called *bar* or *cross stroke*.

Cross Stroke
see Cross Bar.

V

Crotch
The point where two strokes or stems of a letterform meet at an angle, as in a k, v, and w.

y

Descender
The part of a lowercase letterform that falls below the body of the letterform or baseline, as in a g, j, p, q, and y.

a

Double-Story
A lowercase a with a closed bowl and stem with a finial arm, or a lowercase g with a closed bowl and ear located above a linked loop.

g

Ear
A small projecting stroke of a letterform sometimes attached to the bowl of a lowercase g or the stem of a lowercase r.

e

Eye
The enclosed part, or counter, of the lowercase e. See also *bowl*.

Fillet
see Bracket.

5

Flag
A horizontal stroke on the numeral 5.

Foot
The base of a letterform, which normally sits upon a baseline.

Y

Fork
The intersection point within a letterform where one stroke splits into two strokes as in a Y.

h

Hairline
The thinnest of line weights that can be reproduced in printing; also refers to the thinner, curved strokes usually located on the stress or axis of Modern typefaces.

DIDOT (1799)

K

Joint
The angle formed where two strokes of a letterform meet or intersect, as in a K or R.

k

Leg
A projecting diagonal stem or stroke of a letterform extending downward, as in an R and K. Also called *tail*.

fj

Ligature
A stem or stroke that connects two or more letterforms together that form a ligature, tied letterform, or single glyph, as in fi and fl.

g

Link
A stem or stroke that connects the bowl and the loop of a g.

g

Loop
The counter or descender of a lowercase, double-story g when it is entirely enclosed.

V

Overhang
An ascender that extends into the space of a previous or subsequent letterform as with f, *f*, F, T, and V.

s

Overshoot
The rounded or pointed feature of a letterform which extends slightly over a baseline, x-height, or cap line to optically align with another letterform that has straight features. This extension occurs with A, a, C, c, d, e, G, g, m, n, O, o, P, p, Q, q, r, S, s, U, u, V, v, W, w, and V.

n

Shoulder
The portion of a curved stroke projecting from a stem of a letterform, but not the hairline, connecting two vertical strokes or stems.

g

FUTURA (1927)

Single-Story

A lowercase a with a closed bowl without a finial arm located above, or a lowercase g with a closed bowl, stem, and tail. For example, Futura (Paul Renner, 1927; see page 57) features a single-story a and g.
FUTURA (1927)

s

Spine

The diagonal portion or main curved stroke of an S or s.

b

Spur

A small, pointed projection found at the end of a stem or stroke of a letterform, sometimes located on the bottom of a b, t, or G.
BASKERVILLE (1757)

V

Stem (or Stroke)

The principle vertical or oblique element(s) of a letterform, as in an A, B, L, or V; except for curved letterforms, where they are called strokes.

Stress (or Axis)

The inclination of thin and thick, curved stems or strokes (vertical or oblique) in a letterform, which can be an inclined or vertical stress or axis.

N

Stroke

The main diagonal component of a letterform, as in an N or Y.

Q

Tail

The short stem or stroke of a letterform that rests on a baseline, as in a K or R, or extending below a baseline, as in a Q or j. In K and R. Also called *leg*.

fi

Tie (or Connecting Stroke)

A stroke that joins two letterforms together to create a ligature (or tied letterform).

V

Vertex

The lower point of a letterform where stems of a character meet to form a junction with an angle of less than ninety degrees, for example, at the base of a capital V.

Key Typographic Terms continued

Serif Anatomy

I **Abrupt Serif**
An angled connection between a stem and a serif. Also called *unbracketed serif*.

I **Adnate Serif**
A continuous and curved connection between a stem and a serif. Also called *bracketed serif* or *fillet serif*.
BASKERVILLE (1954)

I **Bifurcated Serif**
A serif formed from a main stroke terminating in one or more splits.
MR. DARCY (2014)

I **Bilateral Serif**
A serif extending to either side of its main stroke.
SABON (1964)

I **Cupped Serif**
A serif with a cupped bracket.
JENSON (1471)

A **Hairline Serif**
The thinnest of serif forms as found in Modern typefaces.
DIDOT (1799)

I **Rounded Serif**
A serif with a rounded form.
GARAMOND (CA. 1530)

A **Serif**
The beginning or end of a stem or stroke, arm, leg, or tail drawn at a right angle or at an oblique angle to the stem or stroke of a letterform.

H **Unbracketed Serif**
A serif that connects with the stem of a letterform at a ninety-degree angle, such as in Didot.
DIDOT (1799)

L **Unilateral Serif**
A serif extending to one side of its main stroke.

a **Wedge Serif**
A triangular form of serif.
ALBERTUS (1957)

Serif Anatomy continued

t

Acute Terminal
A terminating stroke that thins at its end without a serif. Also called _tapered terminal_.

JENSON (1471)

t

Angled Terminal
A terminating stroke cut at an angle.

r

Ball Terminal
A circular terminal located at the end of an arm of a letterform, as in a lowercase a, c, or r.

BODONI (1798)

r

Beak Terminal
A sharp terminal that appears at the end of the arc of a lowercase f, as well as in a c, j, r, and y.

CENTAUR (1914)

U

Concave Terminal
A concave termination to a stroke.

OPTIMA (1955)

x

Convex Terminal
A convex termination of a stroke.

GOTHAM ROUNDED (2005)

e

Finial
A tapered, curved terminal of a letterform located at the end of a stroke. Swashes and ornamental flourishes are also called finials.

CASLON (1725)

x

Flared Terminal
A terminating stroke that widens at its end without a serif.

ALBERTUS (1940)

a

Hooked Terminal
A terminating stroke that is hooked at its end without a serif.

CLARENDON (1845)

a

Rounded Terminal
A terminating stroke that is rounded.

BASKERVILLE (1757)

t

Scalloped Terminal
A terminated stroke of a letterform that is scalloped or scooped.

DIDOT (1799)

r

Scutulate
A terminated stroke of a letterform that is diamond-shaped; usually found in Blackletter serifs.

GOUDY TEXT (1928)

f

Sheared Terminal
An abrupt and almost perpendicular terminating stroke of a letterform.

FRUTIGER (1975)

r

Squared Terminal
A terminated stroke of a letterform that is squared at its end.

CLARENDON (1845)

k

Straight Terminal
A terminated stroke of a letterform that is cut perpendicular to its main stroke.

HELVETICA (1956)

f

Swash
A flourished terminal, stem, or stroke added to a letterform.

Tapered Terminal
see Acute Terminal.

f

Teardrop Terminal
A teardrop-shaped terminal located at a stroke end to a lowercase letterform such as f, j, and r in some typefaces. Also called _lachrymal terminal_.

BASKERVILLE (1757)

f

Terminal (or Finial)
The end of any stem or stroke of a letterform that does not terminate with a serif. See also *sheared terminal*.
FRUTIGER (1975)

z

Vertical Terminal
A terminating stroke of a letterform that is vertically cut.
UNIVERS (1957))

Accent
see Diacritical Mark.

ă

Accented Character
Character with an accent (also called *diacritical mark*) for foreign-language typesetting or for indicating pronunciation.

Acute Accent
see Diacritical Mark.

½

Adaptable Fraction
Fraction comprised of three separate characters, where the height of the diagonal equals the height of the numerals on either side. Some typefaces contain adaptable fractions as glyphs, but they can also be created by using the existing characters of a typeface. Also called *built fraction*.

44

Alternate Character
An additional letterform different in graphic form than its standard design. An example is lining figures in comparison to old style (non-lining) figures.

&

Ampersand
A glyph used in lieu of the word "and;" derived from the ligature of the letters et; Latin for "and."

Angle Quotes
see Guillemets.

Apostrophe
see Punctuation Marks.

Arabesques
see Ornament.

Key Typographic Terms continued

Characters and Glyphs continued

Arabic Figures
Arabic Figures, also known as Hindu-Arabic numerals or Hindu numerals, are the ten figures 0 through 9, based on the Hindu-Arabic numeral system which is the most common system of numbers used throughout the world.
THESANS ARABIC (1994)

Asterisk
A star-like glyph used to indicate a footnote or other additional information.

At Symbol
An at symbol is a typographic glyph originally used in commercial accounting as a symbol for "at the rate of;" for example: 7 widgets @ $ 1.00 = $ 7.00. Today, it is commonly used in email addresses.

Backslash
A backslash is a typographic glyph primarily used in computer programming. It is the mirror image of a slash. Also called *backslant*, *reverse slash*, or *reverse solidus*.

Backslant
see Backslash.

Baseline
An invisible line on which the base of letterforms sit or align.

Basis Point
A typographic glyph used as a unit of measurement to indicate one hundredth of a percent, such as with interest rates.

Bitmap Font
A computer font comprised of pixels (square dots) set at a specific size that cannot be scaled up or down in size. Bitmap fonts work with PostScript outline- or vector-based fonts to produce an on-screen display of the original outline font. Also called *screen font*.

Boldface
A font version that is a blacker, heavier version of its normal or regular weight.

Braces
Braces are traditionally used in technical and mathematical writing to identify phrases and sets, and are always used in pairs, sometimes described as opening and closing or left and right. In text settings, they can function as an additional set of inner or outer parentheses. Also called *curly brackets*.

Brackets (Angled or Square)
Brackets, either angled or squared, identify text changes within quoted narrative material and are always used in pair, sometimes described as opening and closing or left and right.

Broken Bar
see Vertical Bar.

Built Fraction
see Adaptable Fraction.

Bullet
A dot or mark located to the left of listed items indicating separate but related points that deserve specific attention.

Capitals
The set of large letters in a typeface. Also called *majuscules* or *uppercase*.

^

Caret
A caret is a typographic glyph and proofreading mark used to indicate where a punctuation mark, word, or phrase is to be added or inserted to a manuscript or document.

Caron
see Diacritical Mark.

Case
The term used to describe a typeface's two case forms—uppercase and lowercase. Uppercase is the set of large letterforms derived from majuscule written characters, which are also known as capitals. Lowercase is the set of small letterforms derived from minuscule written characters. Both of these identifiers come from the era of metal typesetting when they were stored in the upper and lower type cases.

Cedilla
A diacritical mark or accent that appears primarily in French and is used to soften the letter C.

Character
A single typographic glyph such as a letterform, numeral, or punctuation mark.

Character Encoding
An encoding table that maps character codes to the glyphs of a font. There are 32,768 possible typographic codes in the latest font technology, OpenType, designed to accommodate nearly any alphabet system known.

Character Set
A complete group (or subset of a complete group) of characters in a font.

Circumflex
see Diacritical Mark.

Colon
A punctuation glyph comprised of two equally sized dots centered on a common vertical axis, and usually preceding a list, enumeration, or explanation. It is also used with ratios, titles and subtitles of books, cities and publishers in bibliographies, biblical citations for chapter and verse, hours and minutes, and in business letter salutations and formal letter writing.

Comma
A punctuation glyph that possesses the same shape as an apostrophe or single closing quotation mark, and is always located on the baseline of text. It is used to separate parts of a narrative sentence, such as clauses and items in list form.

Condensed
A narrower version of a typeface. Well-designed condensed typefaces retain readability despite their narrower character width.

UNIVERS (1957)

Contrast
The visual degree of weight change in the stroke of a letterform.

Crescent
see Diacritical Mark.

Curly Brackets
see Braces.

Currency Symbols
Glyphs used to identify global monetary systems such as U. S. dollar, British pound, euro, and Japanese yen.

Curvy Quotes
see Quotation Marks.

Dagger
The dagger glyph is primarily used to visually reference footnotes in continuous text settings, as well as to indicate death in those instances when it is located before or after a person's name.

THESANS (1994)

Degree Mark
A degree mark is a typographic glyph composed of a small circle that is located above a line of text and used in both mathematics and narrative text settings to indicate temperatures, inclines, latitudes, longitudes, and compass bearings.

Diacritical Mark
A glyph, such as a circumflex, acute and grave accents, cedilla, or umlaut, added to a character and indicating a variation in pronunciation. Also called *accent*.

Dingbat
A non-alphanumeric glyph such as a decorative bullet, arrow, symbol, or graphic ornament. Also called *Pi Font* or *Printer's Flower*. Zapf Dingbats (Hermann Zapf, 1978; see page 142) is one of the most popular examples of a dingbat font.

ZAPF DINGBATS (1978)

Diphthong
A diphthong is a single character, glyph, or ligature that is composed of two vowel letterforms used for phonetic, rather than visual or aesthetic reasons, such as with an ae or oe.

Display Typeface
A slightly bolder version of a standard text font, traditionally used at larger sizes for display titles and headlines.

EAGLE (1934)

Ditto Mark
A ditto mark is a typographic symbol used to indicate words or figures located below the mark are to be repeated.

Dot
A punctuation glyph in the form of a typographic dot that either is used at the end of a sentence or caps the strokes of a lowercase i and j.

Drop Cap
A large-scale or display ornamental character located at the beginning of a text paragraph that sometimes extends down by several lines. Traditionally used to indicate the start of a new section of text, such as a chapter. Also called *dropped initial*, *initial cap*, or *initial letter*.

Dropped Initial
see Drop Cap.

Dumb Quotes
see Quotation Marks.

Dyet
see Diacritical Mark.

Ellipsis
A punctuation glyph comprised of three evenly spaced dots, or periods, in a row; indicating a missing word or phrase.

Em Dash
A dash equal to the length of one em in width. Used to indicate missing material or a break in a sentence.

En Dash

A dash equal to the length of one en in width. Used to indicate a range of values, for example pages 8-24.

End Mark

An end mark is a small character or glyph located at the end of running narrative text to indicate to a reader the end of an article, chapter, or story. Also called *end sign*.

JENSON (1471)

End Sign

see End Mark.

Exclamation Mark

A punctuation glyph used after an interjection or exclamation to indicate strong feelings or emotions, and often located at the end of a sentence.

Expanded

A version of a typeface with characters of the same weight, but wider than the normal width of other styles within the same font family. Also called *Extended*.

UNIVERS (1957)

Expert Characters

A character set that includes small capitals, old style figures, em-fractions, superior and inferior figures, superior lowercase, additional ligatures, and other specialized characters.

Extended

See Expanded.

Figure

A figure, also referred to as a number or numeral, is universally organized into two primary categories—Roman and Arabic.

Fist

see Index.

Fleuron

see Ornament.

Font

A full set of characters, including numerals, punctuation, and symbols, for one specific typeface in one specific style, weight, and size. See also *typeface*.

Font Family

see Type Family.

Fraction

A mathematical formula comprised of a superior figure, an inferior figure, and a slash mark.

French Quotation Marks

see Guillemets.

Glyph

A simplistic shape, form, or element used to represent a character or symbol within a writing system. This term is also used to describe graphic forms found within a digital text type font set, including letters, numerals, symbols, punctuation, ligatures, and diacritical marks.

Grave Accent

see Diacritical Mark.

Guillemets

A set of punctuation glyphs used in several languages to indicate speech and located at the beginning and end of a spoken word statement. Also called *angle quotes, French quotation marks,* and *Latin quotation marks.*

Hanging Punctuation
Glyphs, such as apostrophes, commas, hyphens, periods, and quotations, that extend beyond the text margin for a better text alignment.

Hedera

The Hedera is one of the oldest typographic ornaments found in early Greek and Latin inscriptions. This ornament, also called a fleuron, was traditionally used to mark the beginning or end of paragraphs, but is now mostly used for page ornamentation. The word "hedera" is the Latin name for ivy.
JENSON (1471)

Hyphen

The hyphen is one of the horizontal line marks used to divide or connect words. When used to divide words, the hyphen occurs at the end of a line length and at a syllabic break in that word. As a connector, it is used with compound words such as pro-active, word-of-mouth, and one-of-a kind.

Icon
see Ornament.

Index

A typographic dingbat primarily used during the twelfth through eighteenth centuries as a graphic indicator directing the reader's attention to important text. Also called *fist*, *manicule*, or *pointing hand*.
THESANS (1994)

Initial Cap
A large ornamental character located at the beginning of a paragraph. Also called *drop cap*.

Initial Letter
see Drop Cap.

Intellectual Property Marks

Glyphs used to identify copyright, registered trademark, service mark, sound-recording copyright, and trademark.

Interpoint
see Interpunct.

Interpunct
a·b

A typographic glyph consisting of a vertically centered dot and used to indicate syllabic separation of words. Also called *interpoint*, *middle dot*, or *raised dot*.

Inverted Commas
see Quotation Marks.

Inverted Exclamation Point
¡

A punctuation glyph used at the beginning of a Spanish text phrase, in addition to an upright exclamation point used at the end of the same sentence.

Inverted Question Mark
¿

A punctuation glyph used at the beginning of a Spanish text phrase, in addition to an upright question mark used at the end of the same sentence.

Italic

A script-like or slanted version of a roman typeface angled to the right and often used to indicate emphasis.
BASKERVILLE (1757)

Ivy Leaf
see Hedera.

Keyboard Mapping
A table defining which character is generated when a particular key or combination of keys is pressed. Also called *keyboard layout*.

Latin Quotation Marks
see Guillemets.

Letterform
see Character.

Lining Figures
see Old Style Figures.

Lowercase
The set of small letterforms of a typeface derived from minuscule written characters, as distinct from capital uppercase letterforms. Their naming comes from the era of metal typesetting, when they were stored in the lower type case. Also called *minuscule*.

Macron
see Diacritical Mark.

Majuscule
The handwritten or calligraphic basis for capital or uppercase letterforms. Also called *capital* or *uppercase*.
CENTAUR (1914)

Manicule
see Index.

Mathematical Signs
Glyphs used to notate basic mathematical equations and processes such as addition, subtraction, multiplication, and division.

Matrix
A brass or copper image of a letterform or character from which metal type is cast. Also used to describe the photographic negative used in photosetting systems.

Mechanical Composition
A typesetting system comprised of a keyboard and hot-metal caster. Developed in the 1880s, this system is best represented by "Linotype" and "Monotype." The Linotype system assembled a line of character matrices and cast each line of type as one piece of metal known as a "slug." The Monotype system cast type as individual letterforms or characters.

Middle Dot
see Interpunct.

Minuscule
The handwritten or calligraphic basis for lowercase letters. Also called *lowercase*.
CENTAUR (1914)

Monetary Symbols
Glyphs used to identify global monetary and currency systems such as U. S. dollar and cent, British pound, euro, and yen.

Monospaced
A typeface in which all characters are allocated exactly the same width and therefore occupy equal space in a line of text.
COURIER (1955)

Monotype
A mechanical typesetting system designed to cast each individual letter as a separate unit or sort. See also *mechanical composition*.

MultipleMasterFont

A specialized Adobe PostScript Type 1 font format that contains two or more sets of font outlines or masters allowing for almost an infinite number of font variations in weight, width, style, and size. See also *OpenType*, *PostScript Font*, and *TrueType*.

Non-Lining Figures

see Old Style Figures.

Numero

A typographic glyph used as an abbreviation for the word "number." It is comprised of an uppercase "N" with a superscript lowercase "o" that is sometimes underlined.

THESANS (1994)

Number Sign

A typographic glyph originally used to indicate the designation of a figure or number. Today, it is commonly used as a metadata tag on social media or "hashtag" and as a button indicator or "pound" on telephone keypads. Also called *octothorpe*.

Oblique

A slanted version of a Roman typeface that is visually similar to an italic version. The term oblique is sometimes used to distinguish sloped letterforms from cursive or italic characters.

FRUTIGER (1975)

Octothorpe

see Number Sign.

Old Style Figures

Numbers that are compatible with lowercase letters. The 1, 2, and 0 of the set align with the x-height, the 6 and 8 have ascenders, and the 3, 4, 5, 7, and 9 have descenders. Also called *non-lining figures*, *proportional figures*, or *variable height old style figures*.

OpenType

A flexible font format developed by Adobe and Microsoft, based on the Unicode standard, that allows for extensive glyph sets and cross-platform use. An OpenType font can be either PostScript or TrueType. See also *Multiple Master*, *PostScript Font*, or *TrueType*.

Ordinal Indicator

A typographic glyph composed of a group of characters that follow a figure or number to indicate sequence or position, such as 1st, 2nd, or 3rd, and are traditionally set as superscript.

Ornament

A non-typographic glyph that includes decorative bullets, arrows, and symbols. Also called *Dingbat*, *Embellishment*, *Fleuron*, *Icon*, *Pi Font*, or *Printer's Flower*.

JENSON (1471)

OSF

A character set for old style figures in lieu of regular figures.

Paragraph Mark

see Pilcrow.

Parentheses
Parentheses are traditionally used for visually separating citations or other narrative asides from a continuous text setting, and are always used in pairs which are sometimes described as opening and closing or left and right.

Period

A punctuation glyph used at the end of a sentence to indicate a full stop to a narrative thought or sentence. Periods are also used after an initial letter indicating an abbreviation such as in "U.S.A." and in mathematics when used as a dot for a decimal point.

Per Mil
A typographic glyph used as a unit of measurement to indicate parts per thousand.

Pi Font
see Ornament.

Pilcrow
A copy editing (or proofreading) glyph traditionally used at the beginning of a paragraph or main section of text. Also called *paragraph mark*.

Pipe
see Vertical Bar.

Pointing Hand
see Index.

PostScript
A page description language developed by Adobe in 1983.

PostScript Font
A specialized form of computer software containing mathematical descriptions, or outlines, of the contours on all of the characters in a typeface. These outlines are size- and resolution-independent and can be used with any PostScript or PostScript-compatible output device. PostScript fonts can also be used with a number of graphic applications to produce various transformations and special effects.

Posture
The posture of a letterform is its vertical orientation to a baseline. Letterforms that are upright and perpendicular to a baseline are identified as roman; letterforms that are slanted or angled are identified as italic.

Prime Symbol
A prime symbol is used to identify measurements, such as feet and inches or minutes and seconds, as well as to designate units in linguistics, mathematics, music, and science.

Printer's Flower
see Ornament.

Printer Font
A digital font set containing data that determines the form of the printed letterform.

Proportion
The proportional changes to a typeface create narrower or wider versions within a typeface family and may include ultra-condensed, extra-condensed, and condensed to ultra-expanded, extra-expanded, and expanded.

Proportional Figures
see Old Style Figures.

Punch
Original metal forms, cut by hand and later created mechanically, from which type casting matrices were struck.

Punctuation Marks
Glyphs used in written and printed matter to structure and separate units (or sentences) and to reinforce meaning.

Question Mark
A punctuation glyph used in many languages to indicate an interrogative clause or phrase.

Quotation Mark
A quotation mark is a glyph always used in pairs with an opening and closing mark to frame a selection of narrative text, either to visually separate titles, phrases, or single words within a text setting; or to emphasize different parts of selected text when they are the spoken word such as with dialogues, quotations, and speeches. They can either be used in a single (' ' or ') or double (" " or ") configuration and are available in two different glyph versions—as dumb or straight quotes (' or ") and as smart quotes (' ' or " "). Also called *curvy quotes, inverted commas, quotes, speech quotes,* or *typographer's quotes.*

Quotes
see Quotation Marks.

Raised Dot
see Interpunct.

Raised Initial
see Drop Cap.

Ranging Figures
Numbers that are the same height as capital or uppercase letterforms and sit on a baseline.
GOTHAM (2000)

Reverse Slash
see Backslash.

Reverse Solidus
see Backslash.

Roman
A typeface style that is upright rather than italic or a regular weight rather than light or bold. Also, the base style from which all other weights of a typeface family are built.

Roman Figures
Originating in ancient Rome, roman numerals are represented by a series of letters from the Latin alphabet, specifically I, V, X, L, C, D, and M.

SCOSF
A character set that includes small capitals and old style figures, specifically small capitals in lieu of lowercase and old style figures in lieu of regular figures.

Screen Font
A digital font set that determines the display of type on the screen. Screen fonts are paired with printer fonts that contain detailed information on each font. See also *bitmap font.*

Section Mark
A copy-editing (or proofreading) glyph traditionally used to mark or number the beginning of individual, sequential sections of running text.

Semicolon
A punctuation glyph used to indicate separation of major narrative sentence elements. Semicolons are also used in lieu of commas to separate items in a list, when those list items contain commas.

Slash
see Diacritical Mark.

Small Caps
Small Caps are usually a feature of expert font sets and include a complete set of capital letters that equal the same height as the x-height of lowercase letterforms. Also called *small capital letterforms*.
JENSON (1471)

Small Capital Letterforms
see Small Caps.

Smart Quotes
see Typographer's Quotes.

Solidus
see Slash.

Speech Marks
see Quotations Marks.

Straight Quotes
see Quotation Marks.

Standard Character Set
Adobe Systems has defined their standard character set as a superset of ISOLatin1. Most other type foundries adhere to this standard. ISOLatin1 is a character set defined and agreed to by the International Standards Organization (ISO). It is the global lingua franca for printed and electronic communications using the Latin alphabet.

Style
In typographic terms, one of the available variations that comprise a typeface family, such as roman, italic, and bold.

Subscript
Characters normally smaller than the point size of body text and positioned on or slightly below the baseline.
THESANS (1994)

Superior and Inferior Figures
Superior and inferior figures are a slightly smaller size than full-size lining figures and are traditionally used when smaller-scale numerals are needed within continuous text such as with endnotes, footnotes, and mathematical fractions. Superior figures always hang from a capline, whereas inferior figures are always located on a baseline. Also called *superscript figures*.
THESANS (1994)

Superior Lowercase
Superior lowercase is a lowercase letterform located above the baseline and smaller in size than adjacent lowercase letterforms.
THESANS (1994)

Superscript
Characters normally smaller than the point size of body text and positioned slightly above the cap height.
THESANS (1994)

Superscript Figures
see Superior and Inferior Figures.

Symbol Font
A font consisting primarily of mathematical symbols rather than letterforms and numbers.
SYMBOL (1985)

Tabular Figures
Numerals that are all the same measured width. Also called *lining numerals*.
RETINA (2016)

Thorn
see Diacritical Mark.

Tilde
see Diacritical Mark.

TrueType
An outline font format developed by Apple and later adopted by Microsoft where fonts are scalable and can be displayed on computer screens and in print. See also *OpenType* or *PostScript*.

Typeface
A distinct design of a type family with common visual characteristics. See also *font*.

Typogram
Type used to visually communicate a specific idea with more than letterforms that make up that word.

Typographer's Quotes
The correct glyphs or smart quotes (' and ") to use for quotation marks or apostrophes, as opposed to the incorrect use of default marks (' and ") or dumb quotes. See also *curly quotes* or *smart quotes*.

Typographic Color
The overall lightness or blackness of a block of text, due to variations in leading, letter spacing, serifs, stroke width, type selection, type size, and x-height.

Typography
The arrangement and aesthetics of letterforms.

U&lc
An abbreviation for upper and lowercase letterforms.

Umlaut
see Diacritical Mark.

Underline
see Underscore.

Underscore
A character primarily used to underline words. Also called *underline* or *understrike*.

Understrike
see Underscore.

Unicode
An international character set proposed in 1997 to contain all of the world's computer code languages. This computer code system forms the basis for OpenType.

Uppercase
The set of large letterforms of a typeface derived from majuscule written characters, which are also known as capitals, and are distinct from lowercase letterforms. Their naming comes from metal typesetting when they were stored in the upper type case. Also called *majuscule*.

Variable Height Old Style Figures
see Old Style Figures.

Vertical Bar
A typographic glyph with various uses in mathematics, computer programming, and typography. Also called *broken bar* or *pipe*.

Weight
The density and stroke width of various typefaces within a typeface family such as light, roman or regular, book, demi or medium, bold, heavy, extra bold, and black.

Widow
A single word or line of text at the beginning of a paragraph located at the bottom of a page or column of text.

Wingding
see Dingbat.

X-height
The height of a lowercase letter, specifically the measured distance from the baseline to the top of the lowercase x.

Agate
A standard unit of typographic measurement in the printing industry equal to 5.5 points (1.81 mm).

Alignment
The organization and positioning of lines of continuous text in relation to a fixed margin or axis. Alignment options are flush (ranged), justified, or centered. Flush left is where all lines start at the same left-hand vertical axis or margin (also referred to as left-justified or ragged right); flush right is where all lines end at the same right-hand vertical axis or margin (also referred to as right-justified or ragged left); justified is where alignment occurs on both left and right margins of the text block); and centered is where all lines have the same central vertical axis no matter what their length.

Alley
see Column Gutter.

Body Copy
see Body Text.

Body Size
The point size of a font, originating from the height of the metal block used to set hand-composed characters. This includes ascenders and descenders, plus the white space located above and below them. See also *point size*.

Body Text
Body text is the main text of a document, distinct from other type elements such as titles and subheads; set in the same font, in the same size, with the same leading, and within the same column width. The body text should be set in a legible style and size, typically between 6 and 14 points. Also called *body copy*, *body type*, or *text type*.

Body Type
see Body Text.

Cap Height
The distance measured from a baseline to the top of a capital or uppercase letterform.

Cap Height Line
An imaginary line that marks the height of a capital or uppercase letterform.

Centered
see Alignment.

Centimeter
A standard unit of length measurement in the metric system; one inch equals 2.54 centimeters.

Cicero
A European typographic unit of measurement equal to the British or American pica 4.512 mm (0.178 inches). A cicero is also equal to twelve (12) Didot points.

Colophon
A colophon is a page located traditionally at the back of a book or publication defining the book's or publication's creation. This information may include background information, facts, dates, and specifications on its production, designers, printers, paper, and typography.

Color
The monochromatic visual density of black, grey, and white created by the massing of a block of text on a page. The choice of typeface, size, weight, line length, leading, tracking, and other factors affect the color of type.

Column Gutter
The space between two columns of type. Also called *alley*.

Column Width
see Measure.

Copyfitting
A process of adjusting the size and spacing of type to fit within a defined area or on a set number of pages. This can be achieved by either calculation, or by successive adjustments on screen until a fit is reached.

Didot
A historic European typographic unit of measurement equal to 0.0148 inches (0.0376 cm).

Em
A common square unit of measurement in typography equal to the size of a typeface's point size. Traditionally, the width of the font's widest letter, invariably the uppercase M.

Em Space
A spatial unit of measurement in typography equal to the size of a typeface's point size. Traditionally, the width of the font's widest letter, invariably the uppercase M.

En
A common unit of measurement in typography equal to half the width of an em or em space or the width of an en.

En Space
A spatial unit of measurement in typography equal to half the size of a typeface's point size. Traditionally, half the width of the font's widest letter, invariably the uppercase M.

Flush Left
see Alignment.

Flush Right
see Alignment.

Greeking
The use of dummy text (often Lorem Ipsum or Latin) to indicate where real text will ultimately appear in a layout. Also refers to gray bars that represent text too small to be displayed legibly on screen.

Hanging Indent
The first line of a paragraph that is set outside the margin used for the remainder of the text. Also called *outdent*.

Hyphenation
The point where a word is broken at the end of a line in continuous text and a hyphen is inserted.

Hyphenation and Justification
The adjustment and specification of hyphenation and word spacing for justified type. Also called *H&J*.

Indent
A space indicating the beginning of a new paragraph in running text by insetting the first word.

Justification
A text setting where lines are equal in length and aligned to both left and right margins of a column. See also *alignment*.

Kern
Any part of a letterform that extends to the left and/or right of the unit width.

Kerning
The adjustment of horizontal space located between pairs of individual characters. Also called *letter spacing* or *tracking*.

Va

Kern Pairs
A built-in adjustment to the spacing of problematic pairs of letterforms, such as Ty, Ye, Va, or YA, incorporated in the design of the font. A well-designed font contains embedded information that defines correct kerning for character pairings that need special attention.

Leading
The adjustable vertical space located between lines of type, specified as a measurement in points from baseline to baseline. Leading is a term that originates from hot-metal printing, when strips of lead were placed between lines of type to provide sufficient spacing. Also called *line spacing*.

Legibility
The measure of how easy or difficult it is to distinguish one letterform of a typeface from another through the physical characteristics inherent in a particular typeface. See also *readability*.

Letter spacing
The adjustable space located between letterforms, adjusted unilaterally rather than individually. See also *tracking*.

Line Length
see **Measure**.

Line Measure
see **Measure**.

Line Spacing
see **Leading**.

Margin
The negative space located between columns of type and the edge of the page.

Meanline
An imaginary line that establishes the height of the body of lowercase letterforms.

Measure
The length of a line of a column of type, based on either inches, centimeters, points, or picas. Also called *column width, line length,* or *line measure*.

Orphan
A single word or a short line of text at the end of a paragraph located at the top of a page or column of text.

Outdent
see **Hanging Indent**.

Pica
A typographic unit of measurement where twelve (12) points equal one (1) pica (¹⁄₆ inch or 0.166 inch) and six (6) picas equal one (1) inch (0.996 inch).

Point
The smallest typographic unit of measurement where one (1) point equals 0.0139 inches (0.0353 cm); also used to define type size and leading.

Point Size
The height of the body of a typeface, measured as the distance from the top of the tallest ascender to the bottom of the lowest descender. See also *body size*.

Rag
An irregular or uneven margin for a vertical column of text.

Ragged Left
see **Alignment**.

Ragged Right
see **Alignment**.

Ranged Left
see **Alignment**.

Ranged Right
see **Alignment**.

Readability
The properties and characteristics of a type block or setting that affect its ability to be understood. See also *legibility*.

River
A noticeable gap of white space running vertically through a column of text.

Running Text

Text set as a continuous sequence of words and not interrupted by other visual elements such as headings, tables, or illustrations.

Text

The main body of continuous copy on a page, distinct from titling and headings.

Text Type

see Body Text.

Text Typeface

Typeface suitable for setting continuous text at sizes ranging from 6 to 14 points.

Tracking

A term used to describe adjustable spacing between groups of letters in text or sentences. See also *kerning* or *letter spacing*.

Type Detailing

Various typographic adjustments that produce visually pleasing and cohesive text blocks such as the elimination of orphans, rags, rivers, and widows.

Type Family

A Type Family is comprised of a limited or extensive group of related typefaces, all interconnected by a set of shared visual characteristics or traits even when their profiles and proportions may vary. While each typeface within a type family is unique and separate unto itself, they all have a strong and obvious visual tie to their base typeface. Initially, type families were limited to only three versions, namely a regular or roman, italic, bold, and bold italic. Also called *font family*.

Unit

A variable measurement based on the width of a letterform or character including white space on either side, not including kerns.

Widow

A single word or a short line of text at the end of a paragraph located at the bottom of a page or column of text.

Word Spacing

The space between words, ideally equivalent to the width of a lowercase i.

Test your Knowledge

1. What is the outer point of a letterform called where two diagonal stems or strokes meet, such as at the highest point of an A or M or at the bottom of an M?

2. What is the area called that is either fully or partially enclosed by a bowl or a cross bar of a letterform, as in an a, b, p, o, or A?

3. Identify the two letterforms found in many typefaces that can be either single-story or double story.

4. What is the adjustable vertical space called that is located between lines of type, and specified as a measurement in points from baseline to baseline?

5. What are other names for a minuscule and majuscule?

6. Identify three (3) primary visual characteristics of Old Style typefaces.

7. Identify three (3) primary visual characteristics of Transitional typefaces.

8. Identify three (3) primary visual characteristics of Modern typefaces.

9. What is the measured distance from the baseline to the top of the lowercase x called?

10. What is a single word or line of text at the beginning of a paragraph located at the bottom of a page or column of text called?

11. Identify two (2) typefaces that have unbracketed serifs.

12. What is the inclination of thin and thick, curved stems or strokes, in a letterform called?

13. Antique, Egyptian, Egyptienne, and Square Serif are other names for what type classification?

14. Calligraphic, Casual, and Formal are other names for what type classification?

15. What does the term "SCOSF" mean?

16. What term identifies a noticeable gap of white space running vertically through a column of text?

17. What is the smallest typographic unit of measurement called?

18. What is a single word or line of text at the end of a paragraph located at the top of a page or column of text called?

For answers to Test your Knowledge,
see page 228.

Section 3

Characters and Glyphs

 singular typeface (or font) is comprised of a single set of visually related characters and glyphs that include letterforms, figures or numerals, punctuation, ligatures, symbols, and diacritical marks needed for typesetting. A typeface's integral visual characteristics, such as stroke thickness, contrast, alignment, and spacing, all contribute equally to its visual appearance, cohesiveness, and functionality.

A type family (or font family) is comprised of a limited or extensive group of related typefaces, all interconnected by a set of shared visual

Roman

UNIVERS 55 (1957)

Light

UNIVERS 45 (1957)

Bold

UNIVERS 65 (1957)

Italic

UNIVERS 56 (1957)

characteristics or traits even when their profiles and proportions may vary. While each typeface within a type family is unique and separate unto itself, they all have a strong and obvious visual tie to their base typeface.

Initially, type families were limited to only four versions, namely a regular or roman, italic, bold, and bold italic. As commercial needs and technologies evolved, so did typeface families and the versions made available within each family.

Roman

The roman version of any typeface is traditionally identified as the 'base' weight of a typeface from which additional versions are built. "Roman" is used as its identifier, which is derived from the inscriptional lettering known as *capitalis monumentalis* and found on classical Roman monuments such as tribunal arches and the Trajan Column (113 CE) in the Roman Forum. This base weight is also sometimes referred to as "regular" or "book," although the term can also reference a lighter weight of a typeface.

Bold

The bold version of a typeface, including identifiers such as boldface, medium, semi-bold, black, and poster, refers to weights of a typeface that possess a wider letterform stroke than its base roman version.

Light

The light version of a typeface is a thinner version of its base roman version.

Italic

The italic version of a typeface is traditionally a drawn version of its roman version and based on an angled axis, and is limited to serif

ITALIC

BASKERVILLE (1757)

FUTURA (1927)

Condensed

UNIVERS 57 (1957)

Extended

UNIVERS 53 (1957)

typefaces. Italic versions of Sans Serif typefaces are known as obliques, which are slanted as opposed to drawn versions of a typeface.

Italic typefaces were originally introduced in the early sixteenth century as a separate and distinct type category. Today they are an integral member of any type family, used to create contrast, emphasis and differentiation within a text setting. Cursive or script italics, for example Baskerville Italic (John Baskerville, 1757; see page 29), are derived from handwriting and possess strong curvilinear visual characteristics whereas obliques, for example Futura Italic (Paul Renner, 1927; see page 57), possess a slanted stroke angle.

Condensed

The condensed version of a typeface is proportionally narrower than its base roman version.

Extended

An extended version of a typeface is proportionally wider than its base roman version.

All atypical characters found in a typeface that are also not referenced on a typical keyboard are identified as special characters or glyphs. Glyphs are not part of the basic alphabet offering in a typeface and include symbols, nontraditional punctuation, foreign characters, and other atypical letterforms. The glyphs palette can be accessed by using specific keyboard function combinations on your desktop computer (see pages 155–156).

Variations in Typographic Form

Typographic form varies in case, weight, contrast, posture, width, proportion, and style. The consideration of these typographic variables is essential for a graphic designer in creating effective and dynamic type in any given context.

Whether using different typefaces or the same typeface with varying weights and sizes, the effective reliance on variations in typographic forms enables you to communicate clarity, emphasis, differentiation, and distinction to a reader when dealing with different types of content. These variables can assist you in organizing a page into separate information areas or levels, while still achieving a visual cohesiveness in how the overall information is presented.

UPPER

UPPERCASE

lower

LOWERCASE

aaaaaa

THEMIX LIGHT, PLAIN, SEMI BOLD, BOLD, EXTRA BOLD, BLACK (1994)

The extensive range of individual typefaces or fonts available today shares these common characteristics, with only subtle alteration and variation in characters and glyphs.

Case

Each letterform in a typeface is comprised of two case forms—uppercase and lowercase. Uppercase is the set of large letterforms derived from majuscule written characters, which are also known as capitals. Lowercase is the set of small letterforms derived from minuscule written characters. Both of these identifiers come from the era of metal type, when they were stored in the upper and lower type cases.

Weight

The weight of a letterform is defined by the overall thickness of its stroke in relation to its height. Common weight variations in most typefaces include light, book, medium, bold, extra bold, and black.

Contrast

The contrast of a letterform is determined by the degree of weight change in its stroke. Any change or alteration to the weight contrast of a letterform's thick and thin strokes will ultimately affect the optical characteristics of a letterform, thereby also influencing its legibility and readability.

Early aspects of letterform contrast are clearly evident in Old Style typefaces where type designers attempted to reflect the extreme visual characteristics of thin and thick strokes of a scribe's handwritten lettering. As printing technologies evolved, so did the degree of contrast and stress in most typefaces, enabling type designers to create letterforms with thinner and unified stroke thicknesses as found in Transitional typefaces.

CONTRAST

Contrast

HIGH CONTRAST - BASKERVILLE (1757)

Contrast

LOW CONTRAST - FUTURA (1927)

Roman

ROMAN POSTURE

Italic

ITALIC POSTURE

Posture

The posture of a letterform is its vertical orientation to a baseline. Letterforms that are upright and perpendicular to a baseline are identified as roman. Letterforms that are slanted or angled are identified as italic.

WIDTH

Width

CONDENSED - UNIVERS 57 (1957)

Width

EXTENDED - UNIVERS 53 (1957)

Width

A letterform's width is based on how wide it is in relation to its height. Its standard width is based on a square proportion. Exaggerated widths with narrower proportions are identified as condensed or compressed; letterforms with wider proportions are identified as extended or expanded.

Contemporary Influence:
Digital Type Technology

In 1992, Adobe released its first advances in multiple master font technology, which provided type foundries and type designers with a set of digital tools that enabled them to create multiple font variations in weight, width, style, and size. Today, multiple master fonts such as TrueType, OpenType, and PostScript Type fonts contain two or more "master" outline sets that enable any type designer to generate a new type style without compromising the visual integrity, legibility, and readability of the base font's original characters.

In 1993, Apple introduced TrueType or "smart" fonts which automatically inserted specific characteristics into existing fonts such as ligatures, alternate characters, and swash letterforms, as well as providing features such as automatic optical alignment.

In 2016, a new OpenType update was announced by Adobe, Google, Apple, and Microsoft which allows for variable fonts and custom styles to be generated from a single font file programmatically.

OpenType now provides the graphic design student and practitioner with a much broader range of features, options, and possibilities for any given typeface.

PROPORTION

KNOCKOUT FULL FLYWEIGHT (1994)

PROPORTION

KNOCKOUT FULL FEATHERWEIGHT (1994)

PROPORTION

KNOCKOUT FULL WELTERWEIGHT (1994)

PROPORTION

KNOCKOUT FULL CRUISERWEIGHT (1994)

Proportion

The proportional changes to a typeface create narrower or wider versions within a typeface family. Versions range from ultra-condensed, extra-condensed, and condensed to ultra-expanded, extra-expanded, and expanded.

Proportional relationships of individual letterforms are an essential consideration when evaluating a typeface for its overall appearance, as well as its readability and legibility. These considerations include the proportional relationships between its cap height, x-height, descenders, and ascenders; variations between its thick and thin letter strokes; the proportional relationship between its cap height and stroke width; and the variations in stroke width themselves.

Style

The style of a letterform refers to the two basic style categories of serif and Sans Serif, as well as its historical context and type classification.

While there have been many different approaches to typographic design over the centuries, whether driven by societal needs or technological advances, basic typographic characteristics such as the ones referenced above are still used. Well-designed typographic forms transcend history, culture, and geography.

Contemporary Influence:
Proportion and the Univers Family of Typefaces

Adrian Frutiger (Swiss, 1928–2015) was one of the most prominent and prolific typographers of the twentieth century and the designer of one of the most notable typeface families ever to be created—the Neo-Grotesque Sans Serif Univers (1954).

As a young boy, he experimented with invented scripts and stylized handwriting as a negative response to the formal, cursive penmanship being enforced at the Swiss school he was attending. He had an early interest in three-dimensional form and sculpture that was discouraged by his father. At the age of 16, he began a four-year apprenticeship with an Interlaken printer working as a type compositor; however, his love of sculpture and form remained throughout his career and was a strong influence in his typographic design work. During this apprenticeship, he also learned woodcutting, engraving, and calligraphy.

Between 1949 and 1951, Frutiger studied at the Kunstgewerbeschule (School of Applied Arts) in Zurich. In 1952, Charles Peignot (French, 1897–1983) recruited Frutiger for Deberny & Peignot, one of the world's foremost type foundries, located in Paris. At that time, Deberny & Peignot was using a new phototypesetting process and wanted Fruitger to adapt typefaces for this new process, as well as design a large, matched typeface family of different weights. It was during this period that he began to work on the design of the Univers family.

The twenty-one (21) variations of the Univers typeface family have five weights and four widths. At the center is Univers 55, the equivalent of a standard "book" weight. Frutiger also proposed to abandon imprecise terms such as "condensed," "extended," "light," "bold," "roman," and "italic," and instead use a reference numbering system that illustrated the proportional relationships between each variation. At the time, it was a revolutionary concept of how typefaces and their related families could be described.

He also created a visual "periodic table" (see above; page 54) for the Univers family—its vertical axis identifies different weights; any variation beginning with the same number is of the same weight. Its horizontal axis identifies perspective shifts; from extended to condensed with italic variations. Any weight ending with an even number is italic. Roman variations are designated with an odd number; oblique variations with an even number.

With the design of Univers, Frutiger also started a trend in type design toward a larger x-height with lowercase letters proportionally larger to its ascenders, descenders, and capitals. The size and weights of its capitals are also closer in size and weight to its lowercase letters ultimately creating a page of text with visual harmony and ease for the reader.

The Univers family of typefaces is known for its remarkable visual uniformity, which enables you to use all twenty-one fonts together as a flexible, integrated typographic system.

SMALL Large

JENSON (1471)

Character and Glyph Types

Special characters and glyphs are not part of a base font set; however, they can usually be purchased as a separate font set or "expert set." An expert character set includes alternate versions of specific letterforms including small capitals, old style figures, superior and inferior figures, superior lowercase, ligatures, fractions, and symbols.

A well-informed and effective graphic designer knows the specific meaning and appropriate usage for the following categories of special characters and glyphs:

Small Caps

Small caps, or small capital letterforms, are usually a feature of expert font sets and include a complete set of capital letters that equal the same height as the x-height of lowercase letterforms.

The color, weight, and stroke width of well-designed small caps match that of their large cap counterparts, while their overall wider proportions match the lowercase letterforms of the expert font set.

They can be used effectively in a variety of applications, especially where you want strong horizontal lines to a continuous text setting, as opposed to a somewhat irregular setting due to the presence of lowercase letterforms with ascenders and descenders. Small caps are often used for abbreviations

and cross references, as well as for effectively creating emphasis and differentiation in dense text settings.

A note of warning—while desktop publishing provides the means by which anyone can create a small cap version of a typeface, the end result will always be inferior and ineffective since it will lack the integral color, stroke thickness, proportion, and kerning that are integral characteristics of a well-designed small cap font.

Figures

Figures, also referred to as numerals or numbers, are universally organized into two primary categories—Roman and Arabic:

Roman Figures

Originating in ancient Rome, roman numerals are represented by a series of letters from the Latin alphabet, specifically I, V, X, L, C, D, and M.

Arabic Figures

Arabic figures, also known as Hindu-Arabic numerals or Hindu numerals, are the ten figures 0 through 9, based on the Hindu–Arabic numeral system, which is a common system of numbers used throughout the world.

There are two types of Arabic figures available in most digital text type font sets—Lining and Old Style figures:

I V X L C D M

IٱⱯ؏Ɛٯ١٧٨٩·

ARABIC FIGURES - THESANS ARABIC (1994)

1234567890

LINING FIGURES

1234567890

OLD STYLE FIGURES (OSF)

Lining Figures

Fixed-height lining figures, also known as ranging figures, match the height of capitals or uppercase letterforms and always sit on a baseline. These are the most common of all figure versions made available in most digital text type font sets. The term "lining" refers to the fact that the top and bottom of figures consistently line up along one horizontal axis.

Old Style Figures

Variable-height old style figures, also known as non-lining or proportional figures, are designed to possess the same proportions and profiles as lowercase letterforms. They align to the x-height rather than the cap height of a typeface, and have ascending and descending

strokes. For example, the 1, 2, and 0 of a typical old style figure set align with the x-height; whereas the 6 and 8 possess ascenders, and the 3, 4, 5, 7, and 9 possess descenders. Due to these visual characteristics, old style figures work extremely well when there is an extensive amount of numerical data integral to a continuous text setting.

OSF is the acronym used to identify the character set specific to old style figures in lieu of lining figures.

Depending upon the digital text type font set selected, as well as the context in which figures are being used, proportional and tabular figure-spacing formats, as well as superior and inferior figure-spacing formats, require other critical considerations.

1079.11
358.23

PROPORTIONAL FIGURE SPACING

1079.11
358.23

TABULAR FIGURE SPACING

1234 1234

SUPERIOR FIGURES

1234 1234

INFERIOR FIGURES

Proportional and Tabular Figure Spacing

Proportional figure spacing is used when figures are integral to running text. Therefore their spacing criteria are based on the variable width of each numerical character, similar to the variable spacing of uppercase and lowercase letterforms.

Tabular figure spacing is used when figures are integral to a columnar format; therefore their spacing criteria are based on a fixed measured width that occupies the same amount of horizontal space. This allows the figures to be vertically aligned, making them easier to read.

These spacing formats are separate and distinct considerations from whether or not Lining or Old Style figures are appropriate for a specific text need. All four options—lining proportional, lining tabular, old style proportional, and old style tabular—are available in most extensive digital text type font sets.

Superior and Inferior Figures

Superior and inferior figures, also known as superscript figures, are a slightly smaller size than full-size lining figures and are traditionally used when smaller-scale numerals are needed within continuous text such as with footnotes, endnotes, and mathematical fractions. Superior figures always hang from a capline, whereas inferior figures are always located on a baseline.

Ligatures

Ligatures have been an integral part of the history of type and book arts since the dawn of printing and continue to be an essential consideration for contemporary type designers when developing new digital text type font sets.

Standard Ligatures

A ligature is comprised of two or more letterforms in which the stem or stroke of each letterform is either overlapping, touching, or integrated one with another to create a unified ligature, tied letterform, or single glyph. The most common ligatures occur with the lowercase f due to the significant overhang of the ascender, especially when it is followed by i, l, or f such as with fi, fl, ff, and ffl. The majority of these standard ligatures are included in numerous digital text type font sets, whether serif- or Sans Serif-based.

The most common ligature is the ampersand, which was originally a combination of the E and t letterforms, creating the Latin word "et" meaning "and."

LIGATURES

WITHOUT LIGATURES

WITH LIGATURES

Diphthongs

A diphthong is a single character, glyph, or ligature that is composed of two vowel letterforms used for phonetic rather than visual or aesthetic reasons, such as with an ae or oe.

DIPTHONGS

WITHOUT DIPHTHONGS

WITHOUT DIPHTHONGS

Fractions

A fraction is a mathematical formula comprised of a superior figure, an inferior figure, and a slash mark or solidus. Standard fractions available in most digital text type font sets include ¼, ½, and ¾. Expert font sets traditionally offer a more extensive set of fractions and other related character choices in a range of weights that have been designed to be visually integral to a text setting.

SWASH CHARACTERS

$A\ \mathcal{A}\ B\ \mathcal{B}$

MINION PRO (1989)

Swash Characters

A number of typefaces include fonts that offer swash characters as alternates. Swash characters possess a more decorative visual quality than their base counterparts and are designed to be used selectively in an informed manner such as in titling or large-scale display applications. Swash characters may include uppercase and lowercase letterforms, as well as related decorative glyphs such as ornaments and fleurons.

ZAPF DINGBATS (1978)

Non-Typographic Glyphs

Ornaments

Ornaments, also referred to as arabesques, have been an integral part of typesetting since 1439, when Johannes Gutenberg (German, 1398–1468) invented movable metal type. Graphic ornaments and embellishments continue to be used to activate a page, separate and reinforce information, as well as invoke a strong sense of tradition in any page layout.

These non-typographic glyphs include decorative bullets, arrows, symbols, and other graphic embellishments, and are also called Dingbats, Fleurons, Pi Fonts, and Printer's Flowers. Popular examples of contemporary digital dingbat fonts include Hermann Zapf's Zapf Dingbats (1978; see left) and Zuzana Licko's Whirligig (1994).

Other non-typographic, ornamental glyphs include typographic rules and borders, which have both aesthetic and functional characteristics when used on a page. Historically, the use of rules and borders stems from the setting and arranging of text matter in the letterpress tradition, when they were used as paragraph markers and endings to running text or used to form continuous decorative borders framing a text setting that required separate and prominent visual attention.

For visual integrity, the stroke thickness of typographic rules should match the tonal value of the text setting in which they are being used. Additionally, the axis of typographic rules is a critical decision in aiding readability and a reader's easy access of information. For example, horizontal rules are an effective organizational tool for, and

RULES AND BORDERS

HAIRLINE (.25 PT)

1 PT

2 PT

3 PT

DOUBLE HAIRLINE

HAIRLINE AND 1 PT

HAIRLINE AND 2 PT

HAIRLINE, 1 PT, HAIRLINE

1 PT DOTTED

1 PT DASHED

in aiding access and readability of, complex tabular information such as timetables, tables of contents, and statistical data.

Foreign Language Characters

Advances in digital type technology have provided the graphic design student and practitioner with a wider range of compatible typefaces for foreign language needs.

Subsequent to the development of Unicode and OpenType, more and more font families now offer extensive typographic integration, providing for the availability of compatible foreign language alphabets or scripts, such as Arabic, Cyrillic, Hebrew, Latin, and Greek, within a single font family.

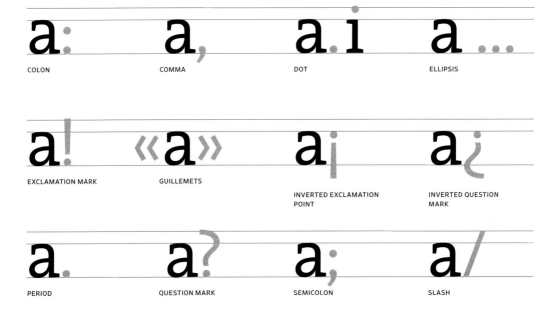

COLON   COMMA   DOT   ELLIPSIS

EXCLAMATION MARK   GUILLEMETS   INVERTED EXCLAMATION POINT   INVERTED QUESTION MARK

PERIOD   QUESTION MARK   SEMICOLON   SLASH

Punctuation Marks

Punctuation marks are defined as any mark, such as a period, comma, semicolon, or question mark, used in writing (printed or digital) to structure and separate narrative units, as well as to reinforce the meaning and understanding of written text. Standard punctuation marks available in most digital text type font sets include:

Colon

A colon is a punctuation glyph comprised of two equally sized dots centered on a common vertical axis, and usually preceding a list, enumeration, or explanation. It is also used with ratios, titles and subtitles of books, cities and publishers in bibliographies, biblical citations for chapter and verse, hours and minutes, and in business letter salutations and formal letter writing.

Comma

A comma is a punctuation glyph that possesses the same shape as an apostrophe or single closing quotation mark, and is always located on the baseline of text. It is used to separate parts of a narrative sentence, such as clauses and items in list form.

Dot

A dot is a punctuation glyph that is either used at the end of a sentence and located on a baseline or at the top of the vertical strokes of a lowercase i and j letterform.

Ellipsis

An ellipsis is a punctuation glyph comprised of three evenly spaced dots or periods in a row to indicate a missing word or phrase.

Exclamation Mark

An exclamation mark is a punctuation glyph used after an interjection or exclamation to indicate strong feelings or emotions, and often located at the end of a sentence.

Guillemets

Guillemets are a set of punctuation glyphs used to indicate speech in several languages and located at the beginning and end of a spoken word statement. Guillemets are also known as *angle quotes, French quotation marks*, and *Latin quotation marks*.

Inverted Exclamation Point

An inverted exclamation point is a punctuation glyph used at the beginning of a Spanish text phrase, in addition to an upright exclamation point used at the end of the same sentence.

Inverted Question Mark

An inverted question mark is a punctuation glyph used at the beginning of a Spanish text phrase, in addition to an upright question mark used at the end of the same sentence.

Period

A period is a punctuation glyph used at the end of a sentence to indicate a full stop to a narrative thought or sentence. Periods are also used after an initial letter indicating an abbreviation, such as in "U.S.A." and in mathematics when used as a dot for a decimal point.

Question Mark

A question mark is a punctuation glyph used in many languages to indicate an interrogative clause or phrase.

Semicolon

A semicolon is a punctuation glyph used to indicate separation of major narrative sentence elements. Semicolons are also used in place of commas to separate items in a list, when those list items contain commas.

Slash

A slash is a punctuation glyph in the form of an oblique slanted line used to represent exclusion or inclusion, division and fractions, and as a date separator. Also called *stroke* or *solidus*.

Quotation Marks, Apostrophes, and Prime Symbols

Quotation marks are always used in pairs with an opening and closing mark to frame a narrative text. Their function is two-fold— to visually separate titles, phrases, or single words within a text setting; and to emphasize different parts of selected text when they are the spoken word, such as with speeches, dialogues, and quotations. Also called *inverted commas, quotes,* or *speech marks.*

Quotation marks can either be used in a single (' ' or ') or double (" " or ") configuration and are available in two different glyph versions— as dumb or straight quotes (' or ") and as smart quotes (' ' or " "). Dumb quotes are default marks found in most digital fonts and always have a straight and vertical appearance, whereas smart quotes are always either curvy or sloped. You should take note that while smart quotes will vary in appearance from serif to Sans Serif typefaces, they will never point straight up and down. Smart quotes are also referred to as curvy quotes or typographer's quotes.

Contemporary Influence:
Zuzana Licko's Hypnopaedia

Zuzana Licko (Czechoslovakian, b. 1961) is the co-founder of the Émigré type foundry and influential type journal *Émigré Magazine*, together with her husband Rudy VanderLans (Dutch, b. 1955).

In addition to producing historical type-faces such as the Transitional serif Mrs. Eaves (1998) and the revival Modern Filosofia (1996), Hypnopaedia (1997), inspired by ornaments and arabesques, became one of Émigré's most popular offerings during the late 1990s.

Each resulting pattern was created by a concentric rotation of a single letterform from the Émigré font library. When multiple patterns are repeated, a more complex pattern composition of interlocking letterform shapes is created. Ultimately, Hypnopaedia provides you with the means by which they can create an infinite number of ornamental patterns by combining and alternating the basic one hundred and forty (140) base patterns provided in the font set.

Hypnopaedia's positive letterforms, as well as the negative space (or white space) they create and that separates each letterform from one another are an essential visual element to the overall dynamic visual quality of each pattern composition.

Apostrophes, also referred to as single quotation marks, have three main functions—to indicate possession, to indicate substituted letterforms, and to indicate the plural of either letters or numbers.

When indicating possession, an apostrophe is used directly after a "s" or a "z" and with or without an additional s (s's). Indicating possession in a plural form, such as when a noun ends with an "s," an apostrophe is added after the "s" but without an additional "s" such as with two designers' portfolios.

An apostrophe also functions as a substitute for one or more letters in word contractions. For example, apostrophes are used as replacements for "do not" when it contracts to "don't" and "it is" when it contracts to "it's."

When used to indicate the plural of either letters or numbers, apostrophes can be used as follows:

"you should always remember to dot your i's and cross your t's" or "in the '70s."

Prime symbols are separate and distinct from straight or smart quotes and have specific functions and usage. They are used for measurements, such as feet and inches or minutes and seconds, as well as to designate units in mathematics, science, linguistics, and music. Prime symbols are commonly confused with single or double apostrophes, single or double quotation marks, acute or grave diacritical marks, and the ditto mark.

"dumb"

DUMB QUOTES

"smart"

SMART QUOTES

'single'

OPENING/CLOSING SINGLE
QUOTATION MARKS

"double"

OPENING/CLOSING DOUBLE QUOTATION MARKS

serif's

APOSTROPHE (SINGULAR POSSESSIVE)

serifs'

APOSTROPHE (PLURAL POSSESSIVE)

don't

APOSTROPHE (CONTRACTION)

4' ½"

PRIME SYMBOLS

PARENTHESES

ANGLED BRACKETS

BRACES

Parentheses and Brackets

Parentheses are traditionally used for visually separating citations or other narrative asides from a continuous text setting, whereas angled and square brackets identify text changes within quoted narrative material. Braces, also known as curly brackets, are traditionally used in technical and mathematical writing to identify phrases and sets. When used in text settings, they can function as an additional set of inner or outer parentheses.

All of the parentheses and brackets shown here are always used in pairs, and are sometimes described as opening and closing or left and right.

one-of-a-kind

HYPHEN

October 3 – 28

EN DASH

—Anonymous

EM DASH

Dashes and Hyphens

Dashes and hyphens are common punctuation marks used throughout narrative text.

The first mark, the hyphen, is the shortest of the three (3) horizontal line marks and is used to divide or connect words. When used to divide words, the hyphen occurs at the end of a line length and at a syllabic break in that word. When used as a connector, it is used with compound words such as pro-active, word-of-mouth, and one-of-a kind.

An en dash, which is shorter than an em dash and longer than a hyphen, is used in lieu of the words "to" and "from" when communicating a range of values, such as a time span or numerical quantities such as October 3–October 28 and pages 8–24. The length of an en dash is always equal to the width of one en (see page 161) and is set without word spaces before and after the dash.

An em dash is the longest of these three line marks and is used to indicate several informational elements in narrative text. It can be used in lieu of parentheses, as well as a colon or comma, if you need a stronger visual typographic element within running text. It can also be used to indicate a break in narrative thought, as well as to separate a thought within a sentence. An em dash is also used to indicate an attribution to a specific quotation and is always located in front of the person's name. For example, "God is in the details"—Ludwig Mies van der Rohe, Architect. The length of an em dash is always equal to the width of one em (see page 161).

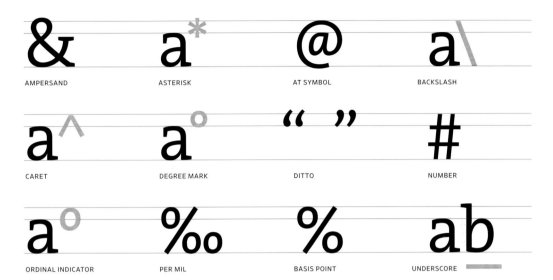

| AMPERSAND | ASTERISK | AT SYMBOL | BACKSLASH |

| CARET | DEGREE MARK | DITTO | NUMBER |

| ORDINAL INDICATOR | PER MIL | BASIS POINT | UNDERSCORE |

Typographic Glyphs

Ampersand
An ampersand is a glyph used in lieu of the word "and," and is derived from the ligature for the Latin word "et."

Asterisk
An asterisk is a star-like glyph usually set as a superscript and used primarily to indicate footnotes, references, or other key words in a text setting.

At Symbol
An at symbol is a glyph originally used in accounting as a symbol for "at the rate of;" for example: 7 widgets @ $ 1.00 = $ 7.00. Today, it is commonly used in email addresses.

Backslash
A backslash is a glyph primarily used in computer programming. Also called *backslant*, *reverse slash*, or *reverse solidus*.

Caret
A caret is a glyph and proofreading mark used to indicate where a punctuation mark, word, or phrase is to be added or inserted to a manuscript or document.

Degree Mark
A degree mark is a glyph used in both mathematics and narrative text settings to indicate temperatures, inclines, latitudes, longitudes, and compass bearings.

Ditto
A ditto mark is a glyph used to indicate that the text or figures located directly above it are to be repeated.

Number
A number sign is a glyph originally used to indicate the designation of a figure or number; "#46" represents "number forty-six." Today, it is commonly used as a metadata tag on social

media, or "hashtag," and as a button indicator or "pound" on telephone keypads. While the number sign can be confused with similar symbols, such as a sharp symbol in music, it is distinguished by its combination of parallel horizontal lines and right-tilting vertical strokes. Also called *octothorpe*.

Ordinal Indicator
An ordinal indicator is a typographic glyph composed of a group of characters that follow a figure or number to indicate sequence or position, such as 1st, 2nd, or 3rd, and is traditionally set as superscript.

Per Mil
A per mil symbol is a typographic glyph used as a unit of measurement to indicate parts per thousand.

Basis Point
A basis point is a typographic glyph used as a unit of measurement to indicate one hundredth of a percent, such as with interest rates.

Underscore
An underscore symbol is a typographic glyph primarily used to underline words. Also called *underline* or *understrike*.

Intellectual Property Glyphs
A graphic designer needs to know the visual standards that apply to the various intellectual property glyphs; in particular, which are superscript when incorporated within narrative text, and which are not. Trademark and registered trademark glyphs are always set as superscript (smaller glyphs located above

INTELLECTUAL PROPERTY GLYPHS

COPYRIGHT

REGISTERED TRADEMARK

SERVICE MARK

SOUND-RECORDING COPYRIGHT

TRADEMARK

CURRENCY GLYPHS

CURRENCY

CENT

DOLLAR

POUND

EURO

YEN

a baseline of related text) in commercial work and are available in preset sizes and heights in most digital text type font sets. A word space should never be added between the text and trademark glyph. For example, Nike™, Just Do It® or Apple™, Think Different®.

Copyright glyphs always appear in line with their related text. A non-breaking word space should always be used between the copyright glyph and corresponding year to

MATHEMATICAL GLYPHS

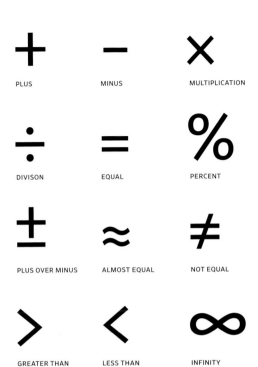

PLUS	MINUS	MULTIPLICATION
DIVISON	EQUAL	PERCENT
PLUS OVER MINUS	ALMOST EQUAL	NOT EQUAL
GREATER THAN	LESS THAN	INFINITY

ensure they do not appear on separate lines or pages. For example: (2017).

Currency Glyphs

Currency glyphs are another common typographic element found in most digital text type font sets and are used to identify global monetary systems.

Mathematical Glyphs

Mathematical glyphs or symbols used to notate basic mathematical equations and processes are included in most digital text type font sets. In many instances, the identifier Pi Characters and Symbol Font is used for a font set consisting only of mathematical glyphs rather than letterforms and figures.

Other Typographic Characters

Many digital text type font sets include a number of unusual and seldom-used glyphs that may be needed depending on specific application and usage. The following identifies the most commonly provided glyphs in this category:

Dagger

The dagger glyph is primarily used to visually reference footnotes in continuous text settings. For example, an asterisk (see page 149) is traditionally used to indicate the first footnote, whereas a single dagger indicates the second footnote and a double dagger the third.

The dagger is also used to indicate death in those instances when it is located before or after a person's name.

Hedera

A Hedera is one of the oldest typographic ornaments, found in early Greek and Latin inscriptions. This ornament, also known as a fleuron, was traditionally used to mark the beginning or end of text paragraphs, but is now mostly used for page ornamentation. The word "hedera" is the Latin name for ivy. Also called *Ivy Leaf*.

Numero

A numero symbol is a typographic glyph used as an abbreviation for the word "number." It is comprised of an uppercase "N" with a superscript lowercase "o" that is sometimes underlined, and traditionally used in names and titles. For example, "Number 46 White Street" is shortened to "№ 46 White Street."

Index

An index symbol is a typographic dingbat primarily used during the twelfth through eighteenth centuries as a graphic indicator directing the reader's attention to important text. Also called *fist*, *manicule*, or *pointing hand*.

Interpunct

An interpunct is a typographic glyph consisting of a vertically centered dot and used to indicate syllabic separation of words. Also called *interpoint*, *middle dot*, or *raised dot*.

Arrows

Many digital text type font sets provide a limited set of directional arrows (left, right, down, up, and left–right) that have integral stroke and proportional relationships to the font set that they are part of.

BULLETS

Bullets

A bullet is a typographic flag or mark indicating separate but related points that deserve a reader's specific attention. While bullets are a commonly used organizational device to draw visual attention to items within a list, they also add visual interest to any dense text setting.

Bullets are usually hung in the left margin of a text column when used in a list, or centered on the text's line length when used to separate larger blocks of running text. In addition to using a typographic dot or bullet, basic geometric shapes such as squares, circles, and triangles, as well as symbols, dingbats, and other decorative glyphs, can function equally well.

Whether using a bullet or other graphic element, you need to give close attention to its ultimate size, position, proportion, and alignment to corresponding text.

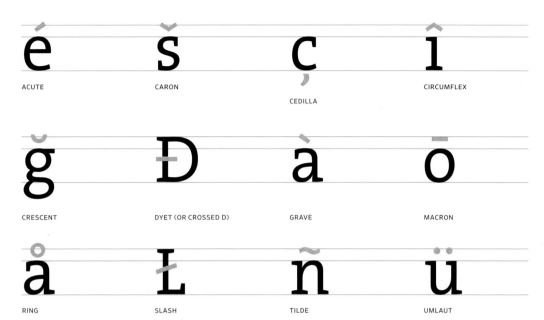

é	š	ç	î
ACUTE	CARON	CEDILLA	CIRCUMFLEX
g	Đ	à	ō
CRESCENT	DYET (OR CROSSED D)	GRAVE	MACRON
å	Ł	ñ	ü
RING	SLASH	TILDE	UMLAUT

Diacritical Marks

A diacritical mark, also known as an accent, is a glyph added to a letterform indicating a change or variation in the pronunciation or sound of that letter or word. Diacritical marks appear either above or below a letterform, or in some cases within a letterform or between two letterforms (usually a vowel or a consonant).

End Marks

An end mark, also referred to as an end sign, is a small character or glyph located at the end of running narrative text to indicate to a reader the end of an article, chapter, or story. These glyph types are traditionally used in magazines, newsletters, and academic journals which have long, continuous articles and sections that utilize multiple pages of running text. End marks can also be used in other non-traditional contexts, such as novels and websites, where a clear and immediate indication of an end to running text is needed.

The graphic nature of end marks can vary from simple geometric shapes such as circles and squares to more elaborate decorative forms such as dingbats, ornaments, and symbols.

Contemporary Influence:
Herb Lubalin and Typographic Forms

CA EA FA FR
GA HT KA LA
NT PR RA SS
ST TH UT VW

Herb Lubalin (American, 1918–1981) was a legendary art director and typographic master who brought humor, sensuality, and a modernist flair to every letterform in his work.

Born in Brooklyn, New York, he attended Cooper Union, where he began his love affair with calligraphy, letterform, and formal typography. Immediately following his graduation in 1939, he joined the advertising agency of Sudler & Hennessey (later Sudler, Hennessey & Lubalin) as an art director.

In 1964 he left the agency to start his own design firm, where he ultimately worked in a broad range of areas including advertisements, editorial design, trademarks, typeface design, posters, packaging, and publications.

During this time he became discontented with the rigid limitations of metal type and began to experiment with cutting and reassembling his own type proofs. Here he was able to explore typography in a detailed and intimate manner that he had never experienced before. He manipulated type by hand—compressed it into ligatures, enlarged it to extreme sizes, and ultimately transformed it by giving it added meaning. It was also during this period that he produced some of the most memorable and dramatic typographic work of the decade.

In 1970 Lubalin joined with phototypography pioneer Edward Rondthaler (American, 1905–2009) and typographer Aaron Burns (American, 1922–1991) to establish the International Typeface Corporation (ITC). From 1970 to 1980, ITC produced and licensed thirty-four (34) fully developed type families and approximately sixty (60) display typefaces including the popular Avant Garde (1970) with its alternate characters and unconventional ligatures (see above). Characteristics of ITC type families included an emphasis on large x-heights as well as short ascenders and descenders, allowing for tighter line spacing—a prevalent typographic style of the time.

Lubalin embraced typographic characters as both visual and communicative forms—forms that were meant to invoke, inform, and ultimately engage the viewer. Rarely have complex typographic arrangements been so dynamic and so unified. The traditional rules of typography were abandoned for a more nontraditional and humanistic approach that made him a typographic master.

A n initial letter, also identified as an initial cap or drop cap, is a large-scale or display letterform (traditionally decorative in graphic form) located at the beginning of a text paragraph and used to indicate the first character of a text paragraph, as well as the start of a new section within running text, such as a chapter. Prior to the

Initial Letters

An initial letter, also identified as an initial cap or drop cap, is a large-scale or display letterform (traditionally decorative in graphic form) located at the beginning of a text paragraph and used to indicate the first character of a text paragraph, as well as the start of a new section within running text, such as a chapter.

Prior to the invention of movable type in the fifteenth century, initial letters were hand-drawn by scribes, who used them to decorate the pages of medieval manuscripts.

While an initial letter was traditionally located above and to the left of running text and appear in a contrasting weight, type style, or color, in contemporary applications location criteria vary greatly. Whether referencing a historical or a contemporary application, initial letters add color, visual emphasis, and typographic interest to any page.

The most common initial letters are raised initials and dropped initials. Raised initials align to the baseline of the first line of text, whereas dropped initials align optically with the top horizontal axis of the first word in the first line of text as well as aligning with a baseline of the running text.

Paragraph and Section Marks

A paragraph mark (¶), also known as a pilcrow, is a typographic glyph used to mark or number individual, sequential paragraphs within running text. A section mark (§) is a typographic glyph used to mark or number individual, sequential sections of running text. Each glyph should always be followed by a non-breaking word space so that the glyph is always linked to the numeric or alpha designation that immediately follows. Without this word space, the glyph and its corresponding reference may end up on separate lines or pages, confusing the reader.

PARAGRAPH AND SECTION MARKS

PILCROW   SECTION MARK

Standard Keyboard Functions

The following standard keyboard functions are shortcuts for accessing specific characters and glyphs in most font sets when using Apple operating systems (OS):

Ligatures

fi	option shift 5
fl	option shift 6
æ	option '
Æ	option "
œ	option q
Œ	option shift Q

Standard Keyboard Functions continued

Punctuation Marks

'	option]
'	option shift]
"	option [
"	option shift [
„	option shift W
‹	option shift 3
›	option shift 4
«	option \
»	option shift \
…	option ;
¶	option 7
†	option t
§	option 6

Question Marks, Apostrophes, and Prime Symbols

¡	option 1
¿	option shift ?
´	option shift E

Dashes and Hyphens

–	option –
—	option shift –

Intellectual Property Glyphs

®	option r
©	option g
™	option @

Currency Glyphs

€	option shift @
¢	option $
£	option #
¥	option y
ƒ	option f

Mathematical Glyphs

÷	option /
Ω	option z
∏	option shift p
°	option shift 8

Diacritical marks

é	option e + e, a, i, o, u, or a
É	option e shift + e, a, i, o, u, or a
è	option ` + e, a, i, o, u, or a
È	option ` shift + e, a, i, o, u, or a
ê	option i + e, a, i, o, u, or a
Ê	option i shift + e, a, i, o, u, or a
ë	option u + e, a, i, o, u, or a
Ë	option u shift + e, a, i, o, u, or a
ç	option c
Ç	option shift c
ñ	option n + a, n, or o
Ñ	option n shift +a, n, or o
å	option a
Å	option shift a

Bullets

•	option 8

Ligatures in Expert Font (Baskerville)

ffi	Shift Y
ffl	Shift Z
fl	Shift X
ff	Shift V
fi	Shift W

Test your Knowledge

1. What is the main visual characteristic of lining figures?

2. What is the main visual characteristic of old style figures?

3. What is the name of the typeface and its type classification that Adrian Frutiger (Swiss, 1928–2015) designed and organized on the premise of a "periodic table?"

4. What is the name of the typographic glyph composed of a group of characters that follows a figure or number to indicate sequence or position, such as 1st, 2nd, or 3rd?

5. What is the name of the glyph that is added to a letterform to indicate a change or variation in the pronunciation or sound of that letter or word?

6. What is the name of the typographic glyph used in place of the word "and," which is derived from the ligature for the Latin word "et?"

7. What is the name of the punctuation glyph comprised of three evenly spaced dots or periods in a row and indicating a missing word or phrase?

8. Identify two of the most popular non-typographic dingbat font sets available today.

9. What is the primary function of an initial letter, drop cap, or initial cap in any text setting?

For answers to Test your Knowledge, see page 229.

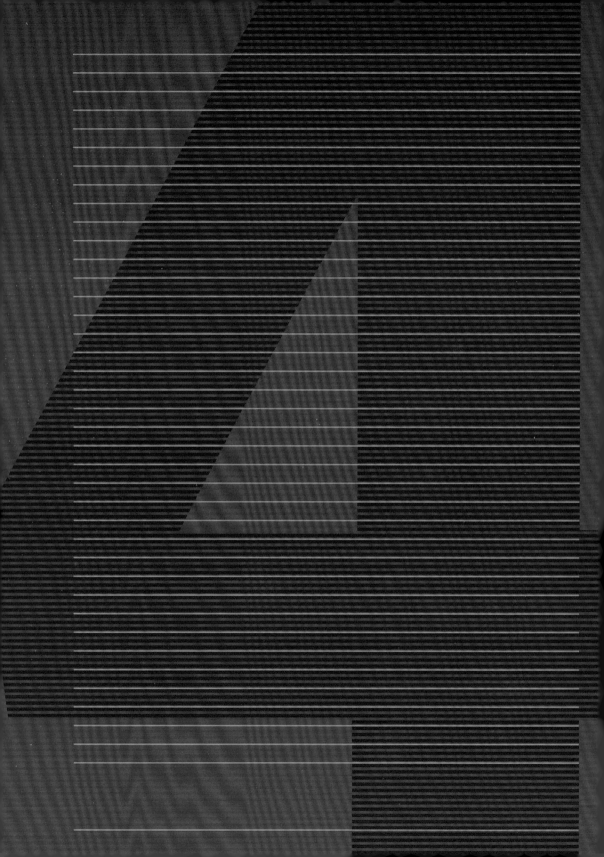

Section 4

Typographic Principles

 ype in graphic design, like written and verbal communications, involves analysis, planning, organization, and ultimately problem-solving. When you write, or speak, you intuitively choose which words to use and how to use them together to effectively communicate your message. With type, the same end result can be achieved; however, a graphic designer needs to be as intuitive.

Typographic principles are the fundamentals relied upon to use type in the most appropriate and effective manner in creating meaningful and understandable visual messages in graphic design. Type is one of the

MEASUREMENT: POINT

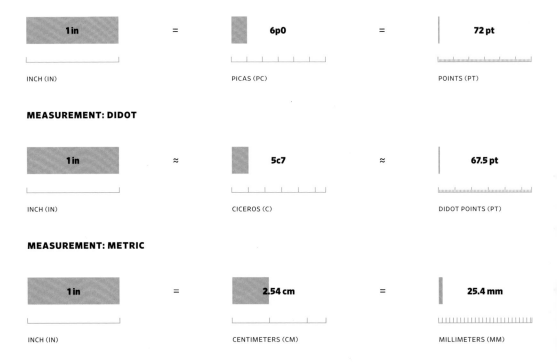

1 in	=	6p0	=	72 pt
INCH (IN)		PICAS (PC)		POINTS (PT)

MEASUREMENT: DIDOT

1 in	≈	5c7	≈	67.5 pt
INCH (IN)		CICEROS (C)		DIDOT POINTS (PT)

MEASUREMENT: METRIC

1 in	=	2.54 cm	=	25.4 mm
INCH (IN)		CENTIMETERS (CM)		MILLIMETERS (MM)

numerous elements, or the "what" of a graphic designer's visual language, and principles are the "how." When carefully considered and used together, they allow you to "speak" in an accessible, universal visual language.

We are taught at an early age about the principles and elements of written and verbal communications. Unfortunately, the same cannot be said for graphic design. However, as we were taught the basics of spelling, grammar, and syntax, we can be taught the same basic fundamentals of graphic design, including the principles of type.

Typographic principles such as measurement, tracking, kerning, word spacing, alignment, readability, legibility, emphasis, and hierarchy are all a graphic designer's vocabulary and grammar for giving voice

and, ultimately, meaning to type in any visual communication. Without a reliance on these principles, type will be ineffective, non-communicative, and will not "speak" to any audience.

Ultimately, your use of typography as an effective and communicative design element is solely dependent upon historical knowledge, technical expertise, and a thorough understanding of the functional and aesthetic characteristics of letterform and typographic composition.

Measurement

There are three primary measurement systems in use today for measuring type; two are based on traditional printer's points and the other is based on the metric system.

Point

The American–British Point System, developed by printer Nelson C. Hawks (American, 1840–1929) in the 1870s, is based on standard units of the pica and the point measuring 0.166 and 0.01383 inches, respectively. There are twelve (12) points in one pica and six (6) picas, or seventy-two (72) points, in one inch.

Didot

In the early 1700s, the use and application of smaller sizes of type were prevalent throughout Western Europe due to advances in printing technologies, which inevitably required a measuring system based on an extremely fine set of increments.

The Didot Point System, developed by type designers Pierre Simon Fournier le Jeune (French, 1712–1768) and Firmin Didot (French, 1764–1836) in 1737, is based on standard units of the cicero and the corps (or Didot point), measuring 0.178 and 0.01483 inches, respectively. There are twelve (12) Didot points in one Cicero.

Metric

The Metric System's standard units are based on millimeters (0.001 meter, 0.1 centimeter, 0.0394 inch). One millimeter is equal to 2.85 American–British points.

While the size of type has always been measured in points, there have been variations in the past as to the precise size of a point. This discrepancy was resolved in 1985 by both Adobe and Apple when they agreed that the measurement of a point would be exactly $\frac{1}{72}$ of an inch so that it corresponded with both Adobe PostScript and Mac screens, which also have a 72 pixel-per-inch resolution. Certain type measurements are relative, rather than absolute, to the point size of the typeface being set. For example, an em set in a fifty (50) point typeface is fifty (50) points. A en is equal to half an em. The following two relative type measurement systems are used to set dashes, fractions, and spacing:

EM, EN, HYPHEN

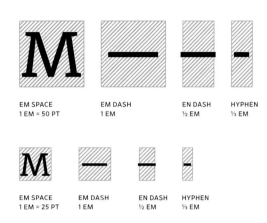

| EM SPACE | EM DASH | EN DASH | HYPHEN |
| 1 EM = 50 PT | 1 EM | ½ EM | ⅓ EM |

| EM SPACE | EM DASH | EN DASH | HYPHEN |
| 1 EM = 25 PT | 1 EM | ½ EM | ⅓ EM |

Em

An em is a unit of type measurement derived from the width of a square body of the cast uppercase "M." An em equals the size of a given typeface; for example, the em of a fifty (50) point typeface is fifty (50) points. It is used for paragraph indents and denoting nested clauses in North America.

En

An en is a unit of type measurement equal to half of one em. It is used in Europe to denote nested clauses. It can also be used to mean "to" in phrases such as, Sections 1–4, and 1975–1981. An en rule is also used to mean "and," between two surnames on the spine of a book.

Hyphen

A hyphen is typically one-third the length of an em. It is used to separate parts of compound words, to link the words of a phrase in adjective hyphenation, and to connect the syllables of a word that are split between separate lines of text.

LINE MEASURE

15 pica ems (2.5 in/65 mm)

Line Measure

The point system can be used to specify a line measure, a column width, or a maximum line length of a typeface. This length is commonly expressed using the pica, a type measurement of twelve (12) points, giving six (6) picas to one (1) inch. This is also sometimes referred to as a pica em, or simply an em. While it is now increasingly common for column widths to be expressed in millimeters, pica ems remain in use as a system of line measure. The line measure used throughout this book can be described as being set 9/14 to a column width of 15 pica ems (2.5 inches/65 mm).

The Em

In the context of line measurement, the term em refers to a twelve (12) point em (a pica), but the expression is more broadly used to describe a measure equal to the body height of the type of any size (based upon the square proportions of a classical capital M). A fifty (50) point em is therefore fifty (50) points in width. Both the em (a measure equal to the body height) and the en (a measure that is half the body height) are used to describe the width of dashes and spaces.

The Unit

The em is subdivided into units. This is a term used for specifying in detail the individual widths of letters and the spaces between them, based on the division of them into fractions. Until relatively recently, it was common for this to be expressed through the division of the em into anything between eighteen (18) and sixty-four (64) units. However, depending on the software used, current PostScript technology uses a division of one thousand (1,000) giving one thousand (1,000) units to the em.

THE UNIT

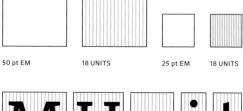

50 pt EM — 18 UNITS — 25 pt EM — 18 UNITS

18 14 12 7 8

Set Width

The resulting type measurement allows for the description of the set width of each letter, that is, the individual measurement of each letter's width. It also provides a means of describing the space between a letter, which can be increased or decreased unilaterally (letter spacing) or adjusted between individual letters (kerning).

Unlike the point, the unit is not a fixed measure, but a proportional measurement based on the size of type used; for example, ten (10) point type is measured in units of 1,000th of ten (10) points; thirty-six (36) point type is measured in units of 1,000th of thirty-six (36) points. Any adjustment to unit values can therefore be applied consistently across a range of type sizes. Letter spacing adjustments are specified in different ways by different typesetting systems, but the 1,000-unit em has allowed for unprecedented precision in the adjustment of letter and word space.

Many current software programs also allow for adjustments to set width, extending or condensing the proportions of the character itself. This should be used sparingly, because any change to the proportions of the letters is in effect a redesign of that typeface.

Metal Type Measurement

Metal type exists in three dimensions and an understanding of typographic measurement began with this early technology. All metal type must be the same exact height, which is called type-high (0.918 inch). This uniform height enabled all type to print a uniform impression onto paper. The depth of the type, which is called the point size or body size, is measured in points. Before the development of the point and pica system, various sizes of type were identified by names, such as brevier, long primer, and pica; these became eight (8) point, ten (10) point, and twelve (12) point. The type specimen chart shown on the next page is reproduced from a nineteenth-century printer's magazine, and shows the major point sizes of type with their old names. Types that are twelve (12) point and under are called text type and are primarily used for body copy. Sizes above twelve (12) point are

called display type, and are primarily used for titles, headlines, and signs. Traditional metal type had a range of text and display sizes in increments from five (5) point to seventy-two (72) point.

As shown, the width of type is called the set width and varies with the design of each individual letterform. The letterforms M and W have the widest set width; i has the narrowest. The length of a line of type is the sum of the set width of all characters and spaces in the line, and is measured in picas.

Spatial Measurements

While em and en are still used as typographic terms, spacing in keyboard phototypesetting and digital typesetting is spatially measured using a unit system. The unit is a relative measurement determined by dividing the em, or the square of the type size, into vertical divisions. Different typesetting systems use different numbers of units: sixteen (16), thirty-two (32), and sixty-four (64) are common. The most important aspect of these spatial measurements that you need to take into account is that spacing influences the aesthetics and legibility of any typesetting.

A graphic designer can measure and specify the spatial intervals of typographic elements within any typesetting. This includes the interval spacing between letterforms, traditionally called letter spacing; the interval spacing between words, traditionally called word spacing; and interline spacing, traditionally called leading (because thin strips of lead were placed between lines of metal type to increase the spatial interval between them), which is the interval between two lines of type.

Caslon I. 1734 Specimen

Metal type specimen chart, 1734
William Caslon
(British, 1692–1766)

Caslon's one-page type specimen chart illustrates forty-seven (47) of his typefaces including Arabic, Coptic, Greek, Hebrew, and Saxon, as well as five (5) page border ornaments.

Optical Issues

The visual character of a typeface has a direct relationship to the perception of its measured size. A typographic line set in the same point size with two visually distinctive type styles will appear to be different sizes. This discrepancy is due to an optical, as well as measured, difference between the actual x-heights of both type styles. Sans Serif x-heights tend to be larger in relationship to their cap heights than serifs, which tend to be smaller in relationship to their cap heights. The difference in optical and measured sizes can vary as much as two (2) to three (3) points depending on the typeface. For example, a Sans Serif Humanist typeface such as Gill Sans (Eric Gill, 1927; see page 63) may be legible and comfortable to read at eight (8) points, but an Old Style typeface such as Bembo (Francesco Griffo, 1495) at the same size will be illegible and uncomfortable to read with any level of comfort or ease.

Measurement System Conversions

Every measurement system can be converted to another related system, based on the following conversion formulas:

1 mm x 2.66 = 1 didot point
1 mm x 2.845275 = 1 pica point
1 mm x 0.0393701 = 1 inch

1 inch x 25.4 = 1 mm
1 inch x 67.564 = 1 didot point
1 inch x 72 = 1 pica point

1 pica point x 0.352777 = 1 mm
1 pica point x 0.938387 = 1 didot point
1 pica point x 0.013888 = 1 inch

OPTICAL ISSUES

The visual character of a typeface has a direct relationship to the perception of its measured size. A typographic line set in the same point size with two visually distinctive type styles will appear to be different sizes. This discrepancy is due to an optical, as well as measured, difference between the actual x-heights of both type styles.

COMFORTABLE - 8/10.5 PT GILL SANS (1927)

The visual character of a typeface has a direct relationship to the perception of its measured size. A typographic line set in the same point size with two visually distinctive type styles will appear to be different sizes. This discrepancy is due to an optical, as well as measured, difference between the actual x-heights of both type styles.

UNCOMFORTABLE - 8/10.5 PT BEMBO (1495)

Spacing

Spacing is an essential and critical consideration when designing with type. Proper and appropriate spacing not only affects the legibility and readability of type, but, more importantly, the overall meaning of any visual communication that uses type as its primary communicative element.

Specific criteria for evaluating and determining proper and effective spacing for letters, words, and lines of text is achieved by the following methods—letter spacing, kerning, word spacing, and line spacing. Tracking allows for the adjustment of spacing located between groups of letters in text settings or sentences. Desktop publishing software programs provide digital features for the detailed adjustment of space located between letters. Letter spacing (see page 166) refers to the adjustment of inter-character spacing applied throughout an entire text

Spacing
TIGHT (-50 PT)

SPACING
TIGHT (+0 PT)

Spacing
NORMAL (+0 PT)

SPACING
NORMAL (+50 PT)

Spacing
OPEN (+50 PT)

SPACING
OPEN (+125 PT)

setting, whereas kerning (see page 167) refers to the adjustment of horizontal spaces located between pairs of individual letters.

Letter Spacing

Letter spacing, also known as tracking, is the adjustable space located between letters, which is adjusted unilaterally rather than individually to achieve an even density to a type setting.

The scale or size of type is a critical factor to be considered when making adjustments to letter spacing. Type set at smaller text sizes tends to lose clarity and visual distinction and therefore may need increased letter spacing to optimize its readability. Larger sizes, such as with display type, may need decreased letter spacing to bring uniformity and visual cohesiveness to the setting.

When using all capitals for any type setting, ample letter spacing needs to be carefully considered to optimize its readability and legibility.

Kerning

Kerning is the adjustment of horizontal space located between one or more pairs of individual characters. Kerning allows for an individual reduction or incremental increase to letter spacing; tracking increases or reduces spaces between words.

For example, some letterform combinations, such as TA, possess visually awkward spatial relationships. This inter-letter space, or letter spacing, can be adjusted, making the spatial interval more consistent with

KERNING PAIRS

Aw	Ky	Pj
Ty	Va	Wi
Xe	Ye	YA

WITHOUT KERNING

Aviator

WITH KERNING

Aviator

Aviator

other letterform combinations. Digital typesetting can be programmed to account for automatic adjustments when these awkward letterform combinations appear. Well-designed kerning creates a consistent visual flow of interchangeable space, which enhances legibility and readability of any typesetting.

Kerning Pairs
A well-designed typeface contains embedded information that defines optimum kerning for specific letterform pairs that would otherwise create disproportionate spaces in any text setting. Kerning pairs, such as Ty, Ye, Va, or YA, require special spatial attention especially when using larger-scale display type sizes.

Manual Kerning
Another letter spacing option is to make manual adjustments to individual inter-character spacing optically, or "by eye," to achieve a more visually consistent appearance. Traditionally, manual kerning is a spacing option relied upon for larger-scale display type sizes, since it is impractical to use effectively on smaller-scale, continuous text settings.

Word Spacing
Word spacing is defined as the space located between words, ideally equivalent to the width of a lowercase i in most small-scale, text settings. With larger-scale display type settings, word spacing can be adjusted manually to achieve optimum visual results.

WORD SPACING

Word space

Line Spacing
Line spacing, also known as Leading, is the adjustable vertical space located between lines of type, specified as a measurement in points from baseline to baseline. Leading is a term that originated from hot metal printing, when strips of lead were placed between lines of type to provide sufficient spacing.

The default setting in most desktop publishing software programs is 120 percent of a specific type size. For example, ten (10) point type is set on twelve (12) points of line spacing (or leading). When line spacing is increased, lines of continuous text appear separate and independent from one another as opposed to one continuous narrative that appears on several lines. When line spacing is equal to a type size, this is described as "solid" line spacing or leading.

Reducing line spacing within text settings so that the space located between each baseline is less than the letter height (also known as negative or minus leading) creates a denser typographic color and risks the potential of ascenders and descenders of most typefaces overlapping one another. Increasing line spacing within a text block creates a lighter typographic color with an open and more accessible appearance.

Typographic characteristics such as x-height, cap height, weight, and type style are all critical considerations for determining the most appropriate and effective line spacing for text block settings. Line spacing also has a direct impact on the readability of any given continuous text setting. Insufficient line spacing creates eye strain for the reader since individual lines of text cannot be read in an easy and fluid manner.

Indents or Line Spaces
Traditionally, an indent or a line space indicates the start of a new paragraph in most columnar text settings. The visual prominence or subtlety of any indent is dependent on the line length being used. A subtle indent is appropriate for a narrow line length, whereas a more prominent indent is better suited for a wider line length. If an indent is used to indicate a separation between paragraphs, a line space is not needed. As such, if line spaces are used, indents are not required.

Another consideration is a reader's perception of a line space versus an indent. A line space is generally perceived as a longer, intentional pause within a continuous text setting, whereas an indent allows for a more apparent narrative flow to any text setting.

LINE SPACING

Line spacing, also known as Leading, is the adjustable vertical space located between lines of type, specified as a measurement in points from baseline to baseline. Leading is a term that originated from hot metal printing, when strips of lead were placed between lines of type to provide sufficient spacing. The default setting in most desktop publishing software programs is 120 percent of a specific type size.

"SET SOLID" LINE SPACING
8/8 PT

Line spacing, also known as Leading, is the adjustable vertical space located between lines of type, specified as a measurement in points from baseline to baseline. Leading is a term that originated from hot metal printing, when strips of lead were placed between lines of type to provide sufficient spacing. The default setting in most

DEFAULT LINE SPACING
8/9.5 PT

Line spacing, also known as Leading, is the adjustable vertical space located between lines of type, specified as a measurement in points from baseline to baseline. Leading is a term that originated from hot metal printing, when strips of lead were placed between lines of type to provide sufficient spacing. The default

WIDER LINE SPACING
8/10.5 PT

Line spacing, also known as Leading, is the adjustable vertical space located between lines of type, specified as a measurement in points from baseline to baseline. Leading is a term that originated from hot metal printing, when strips

EXTREME LINE SPACING
8/14 PT

Traditionally, an indent or a line space indicates the start of a new paragraph in most columnar text settings.

The visual prominence or subtlety of any indent is dependent on the line length being used. A subtle indent is appropriate for a narrow line length, whereas a more prominent indent is better suited for a wider line length. If an indent is used to indicate a separation between paragraphs, a line space is not needed.

As such, if line spaces are used, indents are not required. Another consideration is the reader's perception of a line space versus and indent. A line space is generally perceived as a

INDENT

Traditionally, an indent or a line space indicates the start of a new paragraph in most columnar text settings.

The visual prominence or subtlety of any indent is dependent on the line length being used. A subtle indent is appropriate for a narrow line length, whereas a more prominent indent is better suited for a wider line length. If an indent is used to indicate a separation between paragraphs, a line space is not needed.

As such, if line spaces are used, indents are not required. Another consideration is the reader's

LINE SPACE

Variations in x-heights

A graphic designer also needs to carefully consider spacing variations and proportional relationships in x-heights when establishing optimum readability for continuous text settings. In typefaces where the proportional relationship between their cap height and x-height is pronounced, as in Old Style typefaces such as Caslon (William Caslon, 1725), and Sans Serif Geometric typefaces such as Futura (Paul Renner, 1928; see page

PRONOUNCED - CASLON (1725)

PROPORTIONAL - HELVETICA (1956)

57), more white space occurs above and below the lowercase letterforms. Minimal line spacing or "solid" line spacing is equally effective for these typefaces.

In typefaces where the proportional relationship between their cap height and x-height is minimal, as in a revival Transitional typeface such as Stone Serif (Sumner Stone, 1987) and in a Sans Serif Neo-Grotesque typeface such as Helvetica (Max Miedinger, 1956; see page 51), less white space occurs above and below the lowercase letters. Additional line spacing is needed so that the text setting is easier to read.

Alignment
Alignment formats provide you with options for the organization and positioning of typographic lines of continuous text in relation to a fixed margin or axis. There are four basic compositional alignment formats.

Flush Left
A flush left alignment is set so that multiple typographic lines of text begin at the same point along a left-hand vertical edge. This format creates an asymmetrical text setting

Each alignment format has specific characteristics, as well as advantages and disadvantages, that need to be carefully considered before you select one for applying to any text setting. Alignment formats can have an effect on typographic spacing within any columnar text setting. Alignment formats can have an effect on typographic spacing within any columnar text setting. When text is set in a flush left alignment, word spacing is uniform and even.

FLUSH LEFT

Each alignment format has specific characteristics, as well as advantages and disadvantages, that need to be carefully considered before you select one for applying to any text setting. Alignment formats can have an effect on typographic spacing within any columnar text setting. Alignment formats can have an effect on typographic spacing within any columnar text setting. When text is set in a flush left alignment, word spacing is uniform and even.

JUSTIFIED

Each alignment format has specific characteristics, as well as advantages and disadvantages, that need to be carefully considered before you select one for applying to any text setting. Alignment formats can have an effect on typographic spacing within any columnar text setting. Alignment formats can have an effect on typographic spacing within any columnar text setting. When text is set in a flush left alignment, word spacing is uniform and even.

FLUSH RIGHT

Each alignment format has specific characteristics, as well as advantages and disadvantages, that need to be carefully considered before you select one for applying to any text setting. Alignment formats can have an effect on typographic spacing within any columnar text setting. Alignment formats can have an effect on typographic spacing within any columnar text setting. When text is set in a flush left alignment, word spacing is uniform and even.

CENTERED

with an even left-hand margin and an uneven or ragged right-hand margin.

Since word spacing remains consistent with a flush left alignment, readability is optimum and an even visual texture and color is brought to text settings. While it is not necessary to hyphenate words in this alignment format, it may be needed to avoid extremely long words that create an excessively ragged right-hand margin.

Flush left alignment is also referred to as ranged left, left-justified, or ragged right.

Flush Right
A flush right alignment is set in the same manner with all typographic lines of text beginning at the same point along a right-hand vertical

edge. This format creates an asymmetrical text setting with an even right-hand margin and an uneven or ragged left-hand margin.

This alignment format is rarely used for lengthy text settings since it creates reduced readability and difficulty for the reader in identifying the beginning of each line. Flush right alignments are, however, effective in short text settings such as with captions where a smaller dynamic visual element to a page composition may be needed.

Flush right alignment is also referred to as ranged right, right-justified, or ragged left.

Justified
A justified alignment is set so that every typographic line of text is the same length and

aligns on both the left- and right-hand vertical edges of a column width. This format is the only alignment format where all text lines are the exact same length, creating a symmetrical text block setting with even right- and left-hand margins.

Since word spacing needs to be adjusted accordingly to create even left and right-hand margins, the space between words varies from line to line.

Justified alignment is also referred to as flush left and right.

Centered

A centered alignment is set so that all typo-graphic lines of text are varied lengths with even word spacing and ragged left and right margins, centered above one another, and sharing the same center axis with the width of a column.

This alignment format is rarely used for the setting of dense, continuous text since it is extremely difficult to read due to the lack of a common starting point at the left margin for the reader's eye to orient itself. It is much more effective when used on a minimal num-ber of text lines that occur on a single page.

This format creates a symmetrical text setting and is also known as ragged left and right.

Advantages and Disadvantages

Each alignment format has specific characteristics, as well as advantages and disadvantages, that need to be carefully considered before you select one for applying to any text setting.

Alignment formats can have an effect on typographic spacing within any columnar

text setting. When text is set in a flush left alignment, word spacing is uniform and even. The same effect occurs with flush right and centered alignments.

In a flush left alignment, the hyphenation of words is necessary to avoid extremely long words that create an excessively ragged right-hand margin.

In a justified alignment, word spacing varies because the width of the column is fixed and the words on every line need to align with both vertical edges, no matter how many words are on each line. With justified alignments, variations in word spacing are the most challenging issue for you to resolve properly and effectively. The result of ineffec-tive justified alignments is an overabundance of "rivers"—arbitrary negative spaces that occur and visually connect from line to line within any columnar text setting. One of many ways to solve this issue is to identify the optimum line length for the type size being used prior to creating a justified alignment. Rivers can be eliminated by one of the following methods:

- Adjusting hyphenation and justification set-tings, also known as H&Js (see page 172) in most desktop publishing software applica-tions, increases the number of hyphenations and reduces word spacing.

- Reducing type size achieves a greater number of characters per line. Increasing line spacing creates more pronounced space between each line of text minimizing the visual appearance of rivers; decreasing line spacing makes them more apparent.

Hyphenation and justification, also known as H&Js in most desktop publishing software applications, refers to settings used to create, as well as control, type when using justified alignments. A graphic designer should always take into account that desktop publishing software features and functions are for general application purposes only, and can always be customized for specific results regard-

Hyphenation and justification, also known as H&Js in most desktop publishing software applications, refers to settings used to create, as well as control, type when using justified alignments. A graphic designer should always take into account that desktop publishing software features and functions are for general application purposes only, and can always be customized for specific results regarding design intent, readability, and legibility.

Hyphenation and Justification

Hyphenation and justification, also known as H&Js in most desktop publishing software applications, refers to settings used to create, as well as control, type when using justified alignments. Most of these software settings include the following four options:

- the minimum, optimum, and maximum number of characters occurring before and after a hyphen;

- the minimum, optimum, and maximum number of consecutive text lines ending with a hyphen;

- the minimum, optimum, and maximum word length that can be hyphenated; and

- the minimum, optimum, and maximum spacing between letters and words.

A graphic designer should always take into account that desktop publishing software features and functions are for general application purposes only, and can always be customized for specific results regarding design intent, readability, and legibility.

Rags

When text is set with a flush left, flush right, or centered alignment format, the varied lengths of these lines create an uneven textural edge(s) called a "rag."

When flush left and flush right alignment formats are used, irregular line breaks will occur but can be controlled to achieve a visual evenness. Excessive jagged line breaks are distracting and potentially can create odd negative shapes within text settings, so they should be minimized or eliminated. This can be achieved by either adding manual line breaks or editing the text so that it ultimately creates a visually pleasing irregular shape.

RAGS

When text is set with a flush left, flush right, or centered alignment format, the varied lengths of these lines create an uneven textural edge(s) called a "rag."

When relying upon flush left and flush right alignment formats, irregular line breaks will occur and can be controlled to achieve a visual evenness. Excessive jagged line breaks are distracting and potentially can create odd negative

Optical Alignment

In flush left, flush right, and justified alignments, certain letterforms due to their graphic character and profile may appear slightly indented when located at the beginning of a text line. This will also occur with most punctuation, such as quotation marks.

For optimum alignment, you need to optically adjust or "hang" these spatial idiosyncrasies so that a sharp, vertical-edge alignment is achieved. The extent of this repositioning will vary depending on the typeface being used, as well as its point size. Integral features in most desktop publishing software applications such as Adobe InDesign provide automatic optical alignment functions.

Readability and Legibility

In typographic terms, readability and legibility are interdependent but distinct measures of a reader's interaction and engagement with any type setting. Readability is defined as the measure of how easy or difficult it is for a reader to understand a written text setting. Legibility is defined as the measure of how easy or difficult it is for a reader to distinguish individual letterforms from each other, as well as the words that they form.

Readability

There are four critical factors that you need to take into account when designing type for optimum readability. They are line length or measure, character count per line, spacing, and case.

Longer line lengths or measures create eye strain, causing the reader to lose their place when reading; shorter line lengths or measures fragment text settings, forcing the

"In flush left fl
and justified
certain lette
their graph

reader to become distracted since they are constantly returning to a new line of text. In situations where longer line lengths or measures are necessary, increased leading may assist readability.

Line lengths or measures will vary greatly based on the subject matter and application of the text. For example, in most novels a wider line length is commonly used since the reader has a singular focus and needs to scan long lines of continuous text. In editorial design, shorter line lengths organized in multiple columns of text are more effective for the reader to easily scan information in a selective manner.

A character count of sixty (60) to seventy-two (72) characters (including word spaces) per text line for any given line length is recommended for optimum readability. This criterion changes depending upon typeface selection and type size.

Word spacing is also a critical spatial consideration that has a direct influence on the readability of any text setting. Minimal word spacing makes it difficult for the reader to distinguish one word from another, whereas excessive word spacing causes a

READABILITY

There are four critical factors that you need to take into account when designing type for optimum readability. They are line length or measure, character count per line, spacing, and case.

Longer line lengths or measures create eye strain, causing the reader to lose their place when reading; shorter line lengths or measures fragment text settings, forcing the reader to become distracted since they are constantly returning to

GOOD - 8/10.5 PT THESANS (1994)

There are four critical factors that you need to take into account when designing type for optimum readability. They are line length or measure, character count per line, spacing, and case.

Longer line lengths or measures create eye strain, causing the reader to lose their place when reading; shorter line lengths or measures fragment text settings, forcing the reader to become distracted since they are constantly returning to a new line of text. In situations

POOR - 8/10.5 PT BODONI (1798)

visual separation between words, creating a disjunctive and disruptive reading experience.

Other factors that influence the readability of any text setting include line spacing, case, and the weight of a typeface.

When line spacing is disproportionate to type size and continuous text lines appear separate and independent from one another, readability is minimized. Conversely, when line spacing is reduced and less than the letter height, ascenders and descenders overlap creating a dense text setting that is difficult to read.

Continuous text settings in all caps are difficult to read since they create similar shapes at the same height. Lowercase letterforms with distinct anatomy, such as ascenders and descenders, assist in differentiating words thereby maximizing readability.

Legibility

Legibility is defined as the measure of how easy or difficult it is to distinguish one letterform of a typeface from another through the physical characteristics inherent in a particular typeface.

Legibility is dependent on several factors, including letterforms within a typeface that are easily and clearly distinguishable from one another, thereby making it possible for the reader to assimilate written language with little or no difficulty. The majority of legible typefaces possess prominent graphic features such as larger-x-heights and counters, as well as unique and distinct letterform profiles that make them easily recognizable.

While it is sometimes assumed that Sans Serif typefaces are more legible than serif typefaces due to their clean lines, shapes, and proportions, this is certainly not always the case. Their uniformity and visual cohesiveness presents a lack of visual distinction and differentiation between letterforms, thereby minimizing their legibility attributes for many text settings.

LEGIBILITY

GOOD - BASKERVILLE (1757)

POOR - ARCADIA (1990)

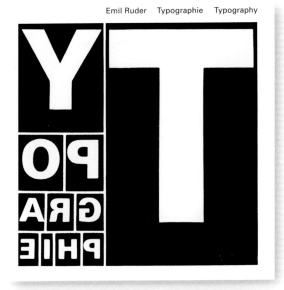

Emil Ruder   Typographie   Typography

Contemporary Influence:
Typographic Contrast

Emil Ruder (1914–1970) was a Swiss typographer, graphic designer, and educator who was instrumental in starting the Allegmeine Gewerbeschule (Basel School of Design), as well as the development of the International Typographic Style, also known as the Swiss School.

In 1948, Ruder met the artist-printer Armin Hofmann (Swiss, b. 1920), and they began a long period of collaboration and teaching that achieved an international reputation by the mid-1950s. Ruder was also a writer and published a basic grammar of type entitled *Emil Ruder: Typography*, which was published in 1967. This groundbreaking book helped spread and propagate the International Typographic Style and became a basic text for graphic design and typography throughout Europe and the United States. Its philosophy and tenets evolved directly from the de Stijl Movement, the Bauhaus, and Jan Tschichold's *The New Typography* (1928).

In his work and teachings, he called for all graphic designers to find an appropriate balance in contrasts between form and function. He believed that type loses its function and communicative value when it loses its narrative meaning. He further believed that typography's primary role in any visual composition is readability and legibility. A careful and critical analysis of visual contrasts, or the contrast of macro and micro, were essential to understanding both of these parameters—the negative or "white" space of the page, as well as the negative or "white" space of letter and word forms such as counters, letter spacing, and word spacing.

Ruder stated, "Typography has one plain duty before it and that is to convey information in writing. No argument or consideration can absolve typography from this duty."

Image: niggli, imprint of Braun Publishing AC ©1967.

Most continuous text settings are comprised of lowercase letterforms, which is another important consideration when selecting a typeface for optimum legibility. Lowercase letterforms vary much more in shape, profile, and proportion than their capital counterparts.

Type anatomy is not only a critical consideration when selecting a typeface (see page 90), but also in establishing effective legibility. For example, ascenders and descenders assist the reader in distinguishing one letterform from another such as j from I or a from d. Lowercase letterforms with open and well-defined counters are much more legible than capital letterforms of the same point size. Additionally, selecting a typeface with a double-story a or g will help further distinguish those letterforms from similar shape letterforms such as o, e, and q.

Design School: Type

Monday, 19 June, 2017
@ 12:00pm

Type is the descriptive term used for letterforms— alphabet, numbers, and punctuation—that when used together create words, sentences, and narrative form. The term typeface refers to the design of all the characters referenced above, unified by common

ALIGNMENT

DESIGN SCHOOL: TYPE

MONDAY, 19 JUNE, 2017
@ 12:00PM

Type is the descriptive term used for letterforms— alphabet, numbers, and punctuation—that when used together create words, sentences, and narrative form. The term typeface refers to the design of all the characters referenced above, unified by common

CASE

Design School: Type

Monday, 19 June, 2017
@ 12:00pm

Type is the descriptive term used for letterforms— alphabet, numbers, and punctuation—that when used together create words, sentences, and narrative form. The term typeface refers to the design of all the characters referenced above, unified by common

COLOR AND VALUE

The weight of a typeface also plays a critical role in achieving optimum legibility with any text setting. Roman, book, and medium weights of most typefaces will generally be more legible than either their lighter or heavier versions.

The most legible text typefaces, such as Garamond (Claude Garamond, ca. 1530; see page 22), Baskerville (John Baskerville, 1757; see page 29), and Bodoni (Giambattista Bodoni, 1798; see page 35), all possess universal visual characteristics that enhance legibility—simplicity, proportion, and contrast. While utilizing these typefaces does not automatically guarantee legible text settings, typographic principles such as measurement, spacing, and alignment will certainly influence how text is read.

The history and origins of a typeface, as well as knowing the type designer's initial intention for its use, are extremely important information when selecting a typeface for a new application. The more information you know about a typeface, the more effective the decisions you will make on any new application for that typeface. For example, a highly legible typeface initially designed for a sign program does not fully guarantee that it will have the same readability when used in smaller-scale text settings. In all situations, you need to analyze, experiment, and develop dummy settings at various sizes and line spacing to effectively evaluate readability prior to making a final selection.

Finally, you need to remember that optimum readability and legibility allow the reader to immediately focus on words first, not on the typeface that you have selected. The well-known design credo "form follows function" by modernist architect Louis Sullivan (American, 1856–1924) is fully applicable in this context.

Emphasis and Hierarchy
Emphasis and hierarchy are related, but distinct, visual characteristics of any type setting. Emphasis is the means by which the

MONDAY, 19 JUNE, 2017
@ 12:00PM

Monday, 19 June, 2017
@ 12:00pm

Monday, 19 June, 2017
@ 12:00pm

T ype is the descriptive term used for letter-forms—alphabet, numbers, and punctuation—that when used together create words, sentences, and narrative form. The term typeface refers to the design of all the characters above, unified by common

Type is the descriptive term used for letterforms—alphabet, numbers, and punctuation—that when used together create words, sentences, and narrative form. The term typeface refers to the design of all the characters referenced above, unified by common

Type is the descriptive term used for letterforms—alphabet, numbers, and punctuation—that when used together create words, sentences, and narrative form. The term typeface refers to the design of all the characters referenced above, unified by common visual elements and

CONTRAST

ITALIC

MIXING TYPEFACES
THESANS (1994), JENSON (1471)

reader can access and engage with an information hierarchy that is predetermined and designed by a graphic designer. This hierarchy includes text elements such as titles or headings, subtitles or subheads, narrative text, captions, and quotes—all of which may require visual emphasis and differentiation.

A well-designed typographic hierarchy provides visual cues that guide the reader through narrative content. When this occurs, it is a further guarantee that the reader will engage with and, more importantly, understand the message being communicated.

Visual emphasis within any text setting can be achieved through creating differentiation with alignment, case, color, contrast, italics, mixing typefaces, position, size, white space, type style and weight, and visual cues.

Alignment
Alignment formats (see page 169) can work effectively in establishing levels of emphasis and hierarchy. For example, a centered alignment communicates a level of importance and is often used for titles and headlines, whereas a flush left alignment creates less emphasis and is often used for continuous text settings making them easier to read.

Case
The choice of either capital or lowercase letterforms is an effective means for creating emphasis and hierarchy within any text setting. Capital letterforms used selectively within continuous text settings create immediate visual differentiation and emphasis. If continuous text lines of all capital letterforms are desired, small caps in select typefaces, such as Sabon (Jan Tschichold, 1964; see pages 26) or TheSans (Lucas de Groot, 1994; see pages 66), should be considered. In both conditions, letter spacing adjustments need to be applied for optimizing readability and legibility.

Design School: Type

Monday, 19 June, 2017
@ 12:00pm

Type is the descriptive term
used for letterforms—alphabet,
numbers, and punctuation—
that when used together create
words, sentences, and narrative form. The term typeface
refers to the design of all the
characters referenced above,
unified by common visual
above, unified by common

SIZE

Design School: Type

Monday, 19 June, 2017
@ 12:00pm

Type is the descriptive
term used for letterforms—
alphabet, numbers, and
punctuation—that when
used together create words,
sentences, and narrative
form. The term typeface
refers to the design of all
the characters referenced
above, unified by common

WHITE SPACE

Design School: Type

Monday, 19 June, 2017
@ 12:00pm

T ype is the descriptive term
used for letterforms—alphabet, numbers, and punctuation—
that when used together create
words, sentences, and narrative
form. The term typeface refers
to the design of all the characters
referenced above, unified by
common visual elements and

TYPE STYLE AND WEIGHT
THESANS (1994)

While an all capital letterform setting communicates a strong sense of formality, it requires more letter spacing, and ultimately, requires more linear space than an upper and lowercase setting of the same text.

Color
Color is one of the most effective visual tools for creating emphasis and hierarchy in any type setting. It should be relied upon in a restrained manner so that it does not create further visual confusion for the reader. When used appropriately, it can draw the reader's attention to a specific location in a text setting or lessen the visual importance of another.

Contrast
Contrast is another effective visual tool to utilize when visual differentiation or compari-son is needed with complex and multilayered text hierarchies. For example, contrast in type size, weight, width, and color, as well as with the location of type within a layout and the use of multiple typefaces further creates visual separation and emphasis to assist the reader. Contrast can draw and direct the reader's attention, create a mood or emotion, as well as reinforce visual emphasis and hierarchy in any complex text setting.

A type composition lacking contrast may result in visual monotony, neutrality, and even confusion.

Italic
Italic type is defined as a script-like or slanted version of a roman typeface angled to the right and often used to indicate emphasis. When italic type is used within a continuous text setting, it allows the reader to imme-diately understand and connect with visual emphasis and differentiation. Italics are also used to convey the spoken word and are traditionally used for quotations or words in other languages.

Mixing Typefaces

Many typefaces and typeface families available today offer a wide range of weights, widths, styles, and character sets that provide you with a multitude of options for creating visual emphasis and hierarchy. Visual distinction and appropriateness need to be carefully considered when using more than one typeface within any given work. For example, the inherent contrast between serif and Sans Serif typefaces may be more visually effective and immediate than using two serif or Sans Serif typefaces.

If two typefaces occur on the same baseline, they will be more visually unified and related to one another if they share a common x-height. This approach will also ease the readability of any text setting that relies upon more than one typeface.

Position

Specific positions on a page layout can emphasize, as well as communicate, an information hierarchy. Different types of information, such as headers, footers, captions, footnotes, and page numbers can have specific locations that communicate their level of importance, as well as reinforcing that given hierarchy.

The activated spatial position of each type element on the page layout, as well as the white space occurring or framing each of these type elements, is equally important to the reader engaging with, and understanding, this hierarchy.

Size

The differentiation of content within a text setting can also be achieved by variations in type sizes. For example, a title, subtitle, introductory paragraph, or pull-quote can be set in a larger size to create visual emphasis. Specific words or phrases occurring within continuous text can also be set at larger sizes for emphasis and visual immediacy, if needed.

The reader's eye will naturally go to the largest-sized typographic element first and then proceed to secondary type-size elements. While you may rely upon conventional locations for titles, headlines, and footers, a well-designed type layout with an intuitive emphasis and visual hierarchy will guide the reader's eye through the correct sequence to the appropriate elements no matter where they are located.

When relying upon this option for creating visual emphasis, you need to ensure that if larger type sizes are needed, type size increases should be a minimum two (2) points larger so that the size difference appears visually deliberate to the reader's eye, as opposed to appearing as a mistake.

White Space

The use of white, or negative space in any compositional layout can create visual emphasis as well as drawing the reader's eye to a specific location. Providing the reader with ample white space reinforces the ease and accessibility of any text setting.

Adding vertical white space in the form of a one-line or half-line space above or below a heading, thereby separating it from the surrounding text elements, can also create visual emphasis.

Type Style and Weight

The majority of typefaces are available in a range of weights—from the most universal roman or book weight that is found in most digital text type font sets to weight variants such as light, medium, bold, black, and heavy. When selecting a particular typeface for a text setting, careful consideration should be given to its style and weight so that it can accommodate a variety of needs relating to visual emphasis and hierarchy. For example, continuous text settings with titles and subtitles may require visual separation and emphasis for the reader.

While conventional solutions traditionally rely upon bold or distinctive typefaces to meet this need, the counterpoint to these conventions, such as the reliance upon lighter versions of the text typeface, can be equally effective when set correctly and appropriately.

Visual Cues

There are numerous ways in which you can create and clearly communicate visual hierarchy and organization with type. When type is used effectively to communicate the organization of narrative content, the reader can easily access this information in an intuitive manner. Visual cues, when used consistently and appropriately in a text setting, can assist the reader in the most meaningful way. Visual cues include indents, line spacing, type style and weight variations, and variations in type size and color.

Indents located at the beginning of paragraphs or informational sections are another simple and effective way of creating visual emphasis within any text setting.

VISUAL CUES

12 PT BOLD	**Design School: Type**
9 PT BOOK	A Practical Guide for Students and Designers
LINE SPACE	
9 PT BOOK (SMALL CAPS)	BY: RICHARD POULIN
9 PT BOLD (SMALL CAPS)	OVERVIEW: Type is the descriptive term used for letterforms—
9 PT BOOK	alphabet, numbers, and punctuation—that when used together create words, sentences, and narrative form. The term typeface refers to the design of all the characters referenced above, unified by common visual elements and characteristics. Typography is designing with type.
WHITE SPACE	
INDENT	
12 PT ITALIC	*"Typography is the craft of endowing human language with a durable, visible form."*
7 PT BOOK (SMALL CAPS)	—ROBERT BRINGHURST, THE ELEMENTS OF TYPOGRAPHIC STYLE

Test your Knowledge

1. What are the two (2) standard units of measurement which the American–British Point System is based?

2. What is the name of the unit of measurement that is derived from the width of a square body of the cast uppercase "M?"

3. Identify the term used to describe the adjustable space located between letters.

4. Identify the term used to describe the adjustment of horizontal space located between one or more pairs of individual characters.

5. Identify the term used to describe the adjustable vertical space located between lines of type.

6. What are the four (4) basic compositional alignment formats that provide graphic designers with options for the organization and positioning of typographic lines of continuous text?

7. Identify the term used to describe the uneven textural edge created by varied lengths of text lines.

8. What common measurement can the graphic designer rely upon to visually unify two or more distinct typefaces when they share a common baseline in any continuous text setting?

9. What are the four (4) main factors that influence the readability of any text setting.

10. What are three (3) visual cues that the graphic designer can use to reinforce visual hierarchy and organization in any text setting?

For answers to Test your Knowledge, see page 230.

Section 5

Selecting Typefaces

hen selecting a typeface for any given graphic design need, there are no universal rules or guidelines that graphic designers need to follow. However, when you rely upon a pragmatic and methodical approach to their selection process, it will guarantee more meaningful and effective results.

The detailed information defined in the previous pages of this book will assist you in making informed and educated decisions about type selection. Without this knowledge base, a graphic designer is pursuing a selection process solely based on a subjective choice rather than on the informed methodology that is the basis for all graphic design.

Ultimately, your final selection of a typeface for use as an effective and communicative design element in your work is solely dependent upon historical knowledge, technical expertise, and a thorough understanding of the functional and aesthetic characteristics of letterform and typographic composition. Without a reliance on these factors, your typeface selection will be ineffective and non-communicative—it will not "speak" to any audience.

By Context

The first and foremost consideration when selecting a typeface must be meaning. Meaning is an essential attribute of graphic design since it is solely dependent on the written word. While type is composed of a series of distinct and unique abstract symbols and shapes, as soon as these symbols and shapes are used in combination with one another to compose a written message, type begins to communicate ideas and resonate with meaning.

When considering a typeface for any graphic design need, your priorities should always be content and context. This fundamental principle is applicable to any medium and size, be it print or digital and small- or large-scale.

History and Type Classifications

With the development of digital typefaces, the number of fonts available to any graphic designer has grown at an extraordinary rate. While it is virtually impossible to become knowledgeable about all of them by name and

The Essential Goethe
Chris Ferrante
Princeton, NJ, USA

Over-scaled, bold typography for this book jacket clearly conveys a historical accuracy and relevance to the book's subject matter by utilizing German Blackletter or Textura. Secondary information in italic and all-cap serif type organized symmetrically on the cover further reinforce the historical context of the book's time period and theme.

by their unique attributes, you should be able to identify the historical origins of specific typefaces, awareness of which can provide insights into establishing strong and meaningful relationships to content. The process of evaluating and ultimately selecting a typeface is complex. A graphic designer who is knowledgeable about the historical origins of typefaces will be better prepared to make meaningful and contextual decisions when it comes to typeface selection.

For example, Centaur (Bruce Rogers, 1914; see page 19) is an Old Style serif typeface that conveys history and classicism, while Gill Sans (Arthur Eric Rowton Gill, 1927; see page 63), a Sans Serif Humanist typeface conveys the opposite—modernity. While each typeface has inherent and distinct visual and communicative qualities, you can use these in either context and convey a specific message of history or modernity. You can enhance and strengthen meaning by understanding the historical context of a typeface. Its history, classification, and formal visual characteristics such as anatomy, proportion, and related nuances are all crucial considerations when going through the selection process.

Typeface selection can also be determined by the subject matter you are working with; therefore this is another reason why the historical origin of typefaces is an essential knowledge base that all graphic designers should possess.

The more background information you know about a typeface, the more effective you can be when evaluating a typeface for a specific application. The history and origins of a typeface, as well as knowing the type designer's initial intention for its use, is extremely important information when selecting a typeface. For example, a highly legible typeface initially designed for a sign program does not necessarily guarantee that it will have the same readability and legibility when used in smaller-scale text settings.

In all situations, you need to analyze, experiment, and develop test settings at various sizes and line spacing to effectively

Credit Suisse
Carbone Smolan Agency
New York, NY, USA
This extensive branding system relies upon a vivid color palette, bold photographic images, rigorous page grids, asymmetrical compositional layouts, and Akzidenz Grotesk (1896), a Sans Serif Neo-Grotesque typeface.

evaluate a typeface's readability and legibility prior to making a final selection.

Contemporary Sans Serif Humanist typefaces such as Frutiger (Adrian Frutiger, 1976) and TheSans (Lucas de Groot, 1994; see page 66) are appropriate and relevant for any modern context, while a revival Old Style serif typeface such as Sabon (Jan Tschichold, 1964; see page 26) and a revival Transitional serif typeface such as Mrs. Eaves (Zuzana Licko, 1998; see page 32) are more suited to classic literary and narrative contexts. Conventional and timeless Old Style serif typefaces such as Garamond (Claude Garamond, ca. 1530; see page 22), Caslon (William Caslon, 1725), and Bembo (Francesco Griffo, 1495) have all been proven over hundreds of years to work well in book-scale text settings, but it is also the responsibility of a graphic designer to consider new approaches and solutions to any conventional application.

Another approach to consider when selecting, as well as combining, typefaces is the historical context of a given subject.

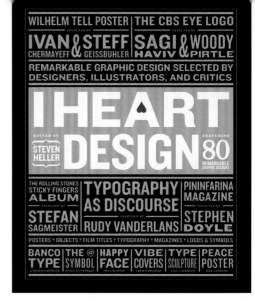

I Heart Design
Landers Miller Design
Portland, OR, USA
This book cover uses Knockout (Jonathan Hoefler, 1990), a Sans Serif Grotesque typeface in various-sized, all-cap groupings, creating a highly dramatic and bold treatment inspired by the typographic vernacular of vaudeville posters, which used American wood types of the nineteenth century.

OzHarvest 2015
Frost* Collective
Sydney, NSW, AUS
The unconventional use of Frankfurter (Nic Belshaw, 1978), a Decorative Sans Serif display typeface with distinctive rounded terminals, combined with a tight, all cap setting establishes a friendly visual spirit throughout both print and digital applications of this annual report.

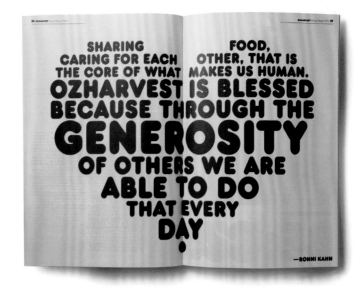

brewster
murray

Brewster Murray
Frost* Collective
Sydney, NSW, AUS

This brand identity is based on the use of a single letterform that when oriented vertically communicates the duality of the BM mark. This simple, yet innovative, solution reinforces an intelligence and resourcefulness with the use of a seminal Sans Serif Neo-Grotesque typeface—Helvetica (Max Miedinger, 1956).

for any given project is to have a clear and familiar understanding of its content, purpose, and ultimate application. Will the selected typeface be used in strictly print or digital media? Will the content require a wide range of weights, styles, and proportions? If the content requires a variety of numerical data and fractions, does the typeface offer an extensive expert set of alternate characters? Will it be used in text scale, display scale, or large scale for environmental graphics? All of these questions, and more, need to be answered first before you commit to a selection and design direction with any typeface. Remember, the application of the selected typeface will ultimately dictate its usefulness and timelessness in any context.

Choosing a typeface that is historically relevant to the time period of the subject matter provides an appropriate context for the use of a typeface. While the aforementioned are traditional approaches to type selection, you need to always remind yourself that for any convention that you follow, the same convention can be broken. This is the essential ingredient not only to effective type selection, but also to the pursuit of creativity and expression in the context of graphic design.

Forms and Anatomy
Whether considering different typefaces or the same typeface with varying weights and sizes for any application, an effective reliance on variations in typographic forms enables you to communicate clarity, emphasis, differentiation, and distinction to a reader.

Application
One of the most meaningful ways to determine which typeface you should use

Typographic form varies in case, weight, contrast, posture, width, proportion, and style. Additionally, a typeface's integral visual characteristics contribute equally to its visual appearance, cohesiveness, and functionality. These considerations are essential when evaluating a typeface for use with any type of content and in any given context.

Type anatomy is not only a critical consideration when evaluating a typeface, but also in establishing effective legibility of any text setting. Legibility is dependent on several factors including letterforms within a typeface that are easily and clearly distinguishable from one another, thereby making it possible for a reader to assimilate written language with little or no difficulty. The majority of legible typefaces possess prominent graphic characteristics such as larger x-heights,

pronounced counters, and unique and distinct letterform profiles that make them easily recognizable.

Most continuous text settings are comprised of lowercase letterforms, which is another important consideration when selecting a typeface for optimum legibility. Lowercase letterforms vary much more in shape, profile, and proportion than their capital counterparts. For example, ascenders and descenders assist a reader in distinguishing one letterform from another such as j from l or a from d. Lowercase letterforms with open and well-defined counters are much more legible than capital letterforms of the same point size. Additionally, selecting a typeface with a double-story a or g will help further distinguish those letterforms from similar shape letterforms such as o, e, and q.

ASICS Tiger
Bruce Mau Design
Toronto, ON, CA
ASICS original logotype designed by Alan Peckolick (American, b. 1940) and Herb Lubalin (American, 1918–1981) in 1977 is the basis for ASICS Tiger's new brand identity which merges **the anatomy and geometric forms of the original with a full set of new characters that mix condensed letterform structures with full geometric circles of the "O" and "Q."**

Ending HIV
Frost* Collective
Sydney, NSW, AUS
Key messaging for this public awareness campaign is addressed through the use of word-within-a-word headlines consistently set in bold, Sans Serif Neo-Grotesque all-cap type inspired by early twentieth-century revolutionary posters.

Client Brief
A graphic designer's foremost responsibility is to their client; therefore knowing and understanding your client, their communication needs and objectives, as well as their audience, are all essential to the success of your work. Type selection needs to be specific and relevant to these client-based factors. When type selection is based on a subjective point of view, such as "I like this typeface" or "I really want to use this new typeface," it is not reflective of what a problem-solving graphic designer should rely upon as their selection criteria for any typeface. Knowledge, analysis, and a methodical approach to a specific client brief will always further guarantee successful and lasting results with regard to type selection.

Understanding Content
Whatever the design problem may be, your foremost priority should always be to become familiar with content before you consider what typeface or typefaces to use for that given content. Becoming familiar with content not only provides you with insights into type selection, it also provides assistance with the overall approach to the design of that content.

Audience
Another essential consideration of a graphic designer's methodology when selecting a typeface is the characteristics, background, and needs of a reader or audience. Prior to selecting a typeface, you need to consider several factors relating to the audience for a specific project, namely, the age, background, level of familiarity with content, and related demographic data of that audience group. This information provides you with specific insights and references that will ultimately influence your type selection.

For Visual Harmony
The visual characteristics of a typeface are another critical consideration that needs to be taken into account when selecting the correct and appropriate typeface for any application.

Euphrasiana –
Cathedral in Poreč
Studio Sonda
Vizinada, HR
Continuous narrative text
pages of this monograph
are organized in a
symmetrical, two-column
grid of Sans Serif type
with a justified alignment
and ample leading that
assist legibility and
readability, and is printed
in black on a metallic
gold background for
added contrast.

Typefaces that share similar proportions, stroke weights, x-heights, and cap heights will be much more compatible with one another than typefaces that do not share these integral visual characteristics. When they share these physical attributes, you are further guaranteed that there will be a visual harmony and cohesiveness to the typefaces being used.

Every typeface has its own distinct visual personality and presence. Each typeface conveys an immediate message, attitude, and mood even before you use it in a specific context. As defined in the previous pages of this book, type is primarily organized in two categories—text type and display type. Text-based typefaces possess subtle but essential, functional visual characteristics that have a direct relationship to legibility and readability and therefore are visually more restrained in their visual personalities. Display type, being used at a considerably larger scale, possesses stronger and, more diverse visual characteristics that reflect their broad and varied visual personalities.

Text Type
Text-based typefaces are primarily used for the purpose of continuous and uninterrupted reading such as in literary journals, novels, and dense book-scale text settings. Humanist, Old Style, and Transitional typefaces such as Jenson (Nicolas Jenson, 1471; see page 16), Garamond (Claude Garamond, ca. 1530; see page 22), and Baskerville (John Baskerville, 1757; see page 29) all work extremely well in this context.

The typefaces referenced above, as well as the majority of serif typefaces referenced in *Section 1* of this book, include some of the most beautiful, legible, and well-designed text typefaces in use today. They are primarily based on roman proportions therefore do not have strong contrasts in stroke weights. The stress of their curved strokes is noticeably oblique, a smaller x-height defines their lowercase letters, terminals are pear-shaped, and lowercase counters are small.

Due to the strong calligraphic influence that is clearly evident in their strong axis,

Details
Blaine Pannell (Student),
Adrian Pulfer (Instructor)
Brigham Young University
Provo, UT, USA
**All-cap Sans Serif
Grotesque letterforms,
cropped at the cover's
top and bottom edges,
creates a typographic
frame for a photographic**

portrait, with a content
listing at the lower
portion completing the
frame. A numero glyph
adds a subtle typo-
graphic nuance to the
overall composition.

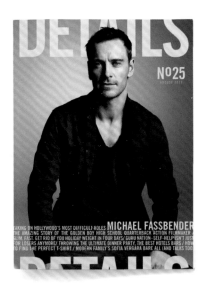

angular cross bars, and characterized by deep descenders, high ascenders, and low x-heights, they require minimum leading. Their relatively small body size, irregular profiles, and minimal counters collectively influence their legibility and readability at smaller sizes.

Display Type

Display-based typefaces share one universal visual characteristic—they are designed for limited use at larger display sizes rather than for smaller-scale, continuous text settings, and are primarily used to gain and keep a reader's attention.

In the eighteenth century, numerous display typefaces were developed by English and French type foundries to meet the new demand for advertisements, broadsides, and posters. As the need for greater differentiation of products and services grew throughout the late nineteenth century to today, an abundance of varied display typefaces, such as Broadway (Morris Fuller Benton, 1929), Entropy (Stephen Farrell, 1993), and Sophia (Matthew Carter, 1993), with a diverse range of visual characteristics continued to be introduced. Display typefaces offer much more variety than text-based type-faces and include a wide stylistic array such as stencils, outlines, shadows, inlines, decorative ornamentation, flourishes, dimensionality, and distortion, as well as typefaces that mimic a wide range of historical visual styles ranging from art nouveau and art deco to modernism, pop culture, and the digital age.

Most text typefaces have been designed with strong attributes of readability to hold a reader's attention whereas display typefaces

Labor
Triboro
Brooklyn, NY, USA

The consistent use of a Sans Serif Neo-Grotesque typeface, Neue Haas Unica (Toshi Omagari, 2015), in continuous narrative text with proportional leading and a justified alignment, coupled with a rigorous page grid, provides optimum readability and legibility for this publication.

have been designed to be used for a minimum number of words and to gain a reader's immediate recognition and attention. In this context of display scale, readability is not a primary concern.

Readability and Legibility

Readability and legibility are interdependent but distinct measures of a reader's interaction and engagement with any type setting. Readability is defined as the measure of how easy or difficult it is for a reader to understand a written text setting. Legibility is defined as the measure of how easy or difficult it is for a reader to distinguish individual letterforms from each other, as well as the words that they form.

When considering the selection of a typeface for text-based applications, readability and legibility are critical considerations. These two factors are also influenced by the typographic principles of measurement and spacing, namely line length or measure, character count per line, word spacing, leading, and case, which are all critical to the success of a graphic designer's typeface selection.

Longer line lengths or measures create eye strain, causing a reader to lose their place when reading; shorter line lengths or measures fragment text settings, forcing a reader to become distracted since they are constantly returning to a new line of text. In situations where longer line lengths or measures are necessary, increased leading may assist readability.

Line lengths or measures will vary greatly based on the subject matter and application of the text. For example, in most novels a wider line length is commonly used since a reader has a singular focus and needs to scan long lines of continuous text. In editorial design, shorter line lengths organized in multiple columns of text are more effective for a reader to easily scan information in a selective manner. A count of sixty (60) to seventy-two (72) characters (including word spaces) per line for any given line length is recommended for optimum readability. This criteria changes depending upon typeface selection and size.

Word spacing is also a critical spatial consideration that has a direct influence on the readability of any text setting. Minimal word spacing creates difficulty for a reader in distinguishing one word from another, whereas excessive word spacing causes a visual separation between words, creating a disjunctive and disruptive reading experience.

A graphic designer also needs to consider x-height, cap height, weight, and type style when evaluating a type selection for any application. These critical considerations will ultimately assist in establishing appropriate

and effective line spacing for text block settings. Line spacing also has a direct impact on the readability of any given continuous text setting. Insufficient line spacing creates eye strain for a reader since individual lines of text cannot be read in an easy and fluid manner.

While it is sometimes assumed that Sans Serif typefaces are more legible than serif typefaces due to their clean lines, shapes, and proportions, this is certainly not always the case. Their uniformity and visual cohesiveness presents a lack of visual distinction and differentiation between letterforms, thereby minimizing their legibility attributes for many text settings.

The weight of a typeface also plays a critical role in achieving optimum legibility with any text setting. Roman, book, and medium weights of most typefaces will generally be more legible than either their lighter or heavier versions.

The most legible Old Style, Transitional, and Modern text typefaces respectively, such as Garamond (Claude Garamond, ca. 1530; see page 22), Baskerville (John Baskerville, 1757; see page 29), and Bodoni (Giambattista Bodoni, 1798; see page 35), all possess universal visual characteristics that enhance legibility—simplicity, proportion, and contrast.

MIDCENTURY MODERN: MODERNISM COMES TO AMERICA

The Stock Market Crash of 1929 started a chain of events that resulted in the G Depression of the 1930s, devastating global economies and putting millions of pe of work. The effects rippled through politics, culture, and society around the wor Germany, for example, financial support for the Weimar Republic from Ameri disappeared, and the Nazi party took advantage of this economic vulnerability as it rise to power in Europe. Designers and artists needed to either conform to Hit or move elsewhere. Many came to the United States, bringing their European sensibilities with them.

Entering World War II helped the United States claw its way out of the Economic Many came to the United States, bringing their European as the war effort created jobs and pumped money back into the econo conflict was over, growing consumer demand and an increase in birth ... fueled an economic surge. Cars and a new interstate highway ... which spawned hotels and fast-food res ...oages for military return ...burban w

Graphic Icons: Visionaries Who Shaped Modern Graphic Design Think Studio Maplewood, NJ, USA **The typefaces used for this publication, Sans Serif Neo-Grotesque Univers (Adrian Frutiger, 1954) and contemporary Old Style serif Scala**

(Martin Majoor, 1990) possess visual characteristics that enhance legibility: simplicity, proportion, and contrast. Several weights of Univers are used for titles, subtitles, captions, and information graphics; Scala is used solely for continuous narrative text.

While utilizing these typefaces does not automatically guarantee legible text settings, typographic principles such as measurement, spacing, and alignment will certainly influence how these text settings are read.

Finally, you need to remember that optimum readability and legibility allow a reader to immediately focus on words first, not on the typeface you have selected. The well-known design credo "form follows function" by modernist architect Louis Sullivan (American, 1856–1924) is fully applicable in this context.

Croatian Design Review
Studio Sonda
Vizinada, HR
This catalog on Croatian graphic design suggests that the book's structure and graphic elements are unfinished. Its color palette of red, blue, and white are taken from the Croatian national flag.

The use of a Sans Serif Humanist typeface that has lowercase letterforms with a pronounced x-height provide additional visual prominence to this cover's type treatment.

Cap Height and X-Height Variations
Spacing variations and proportional relationships in cap heights and x-heights are other considerations you need to carefully evaluate for optimum readability when evaluating and ultimately selecting a typeface for continuous text settings.

In typefaces where the proportional relationship between their cap height and x-height is pronounced, such as in Caslon (William Caslon, 1725), an Old Style serif, and Futura (Paul Renner, 1928; see page 57), a San Serif Geometric, more white space occurs above and below the lowercase letterforms. These visual characteristics require type to be set at a larger point size and make type easier to read, allowing a reader's eye to travel back and forth along text lines without any difficulty. Minimal line spacing or "solid" line spacing is equally effective for these typefaces.

In typefaces where the proportional relationship between the cap height and x-height is minimal, such as in Stone Serif

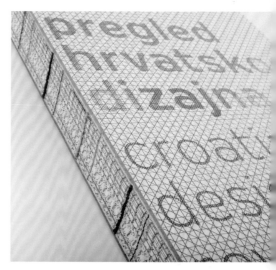

(Sumner Stone, 1987), a revival Transitional serif typeface, and Helvetica (Max Miedinger, 1956; see page 51), a San Serif Neo-Grotesque typeface, less white space occurs above and below the lowercase letters. Additional line spacing is needed so that the text setting is easier to read.

The anatomy of any typeface also needs to be carefully and thoroughly analyzed and compared so that you can make an informed selection of any typeface. Sizes of x-heights and letterform counters, as well as the stress or axis of letterforms, are all visual characteristics of a typeface that need to be compared to one another when going through the evaluation and selection process.

A graphic designer needs to remember that the x-height is the height of the lower-case x in any typeface and traditionally determines the optical size of that typeface. Optical sizes can vary from typeface to typeface. For example, Bodoni (Giambattista Bodoni, 1798; see page 35), a Modern serif typeface, possesses a small x-height in comparison to HTF Didot (Jonathan Hoefler, 1991), a revival Modern serif typeface which possesses a larger x-height. While each typeface has the same body size, typefaces with larger x-heights have small ascenders and descenders while typefaces with smaller x-heights have larger ones.

Contrast

When using more than one typeface, combinations that rely upon the visual principle of contrast will clearly communicate hierarchy in a much more immediate and understandable manner to a reader. Contrast provides you with a means by which continuous text

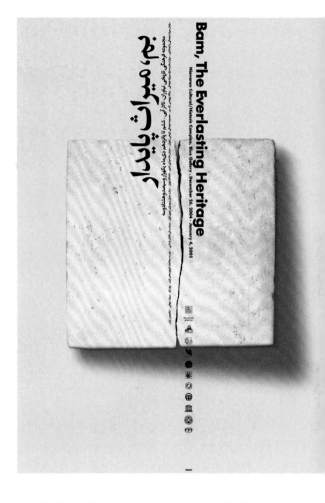

Bam, The Everlasting Heritage
Majid Abassi
Tehran, IR
The use of a highly-nuanced and calligraphic-based Arabic typeface coupled with the rigorous structure of the Sans Serif Geometric Futura (Paul Renner, 1927) typeface provides an immediate and obvious visual contrast, as well as an appropriate typographic identity, for this promotional poster announcing an exhibition and conference on the potential renovation of the legendary city of Bam, one of the world's most famous architectural landmarks, located in southern Iran.

JFK Terminal 4
Base Design
New York, NY, USA
This brand identity's logotype and custom Sans Serif type is paired with vibrant colors on a bright white background in a variety of scale applications—

from wall murals and digital directories to retail corridor walls and gate graphics. Program elements are equally effective in large-scale environmental graphics as well as in small-scale print and digital applications.

settings or paragraphs are separate and distinct from their organizational information elements, such as headings and subheadings. The effective use of contrast provides a reader with a clear indication of what your intent is— where should the attention and the eye of a reader go first, second, third, and so on.

When pairing typefaces is an option, you should always consider contrasting visual characteristics between the two or more typefaces being considered, as compared to their similar visual characteristics. For example, the pairing of Helvetica (Max Miedinger, 1956; see page 51) and Arial (Robin Nicholas, Patricia Saunders, 1982), both San Serif Neo-Grotesque typefaces, in a small-scale text setting provides a reader with subtle similarities as opposed to obvious differences between the two typefaces. When similarities are subtle, it leads to confusion rather than clarity for a reader.

Contrast can also be achieved in text settings by using one typeface family that offers an extensive range of weights, sizes, and styles to achieve varied type color and density such as Thesis (Lucas de Groot, 1994; see page 67) or AgroSans (Lucas de Groot, 1997), both revival Sans Serif Humanist typefaces. Other visual factors such as leading, interparagraph spacing, indents, and letter spacing are also critical in creating functional and apparent contrast in text settings.

Size
Type size is a critical consideration when evaluating and selecting typefaces for any application. Not all typefaces function equally and effectively at the same size, so the more you can estimate final type sizes, line lengths or measures, leading, and spacing prior to committing to any typeface the more informed the final type selection will be. For example, using a specific typeface in a

book-scale text setting or in larger-scale wall graphics is a consideration to be taken into account before committing to any typeface selection.

In certain situations, you may want to consider a broader family of typefaces to meet the diversity of need due to the final size and application. In either case, type foundries are a great resource for any graphic designer to refer to for understanding typeface specifications, size criteria, sample applications, and design guidelines for potential end use.

Low-Resolution Applications
When evaluating typefaces for low-resolution applications, a graphic designer should consider typefaces that have a web-based font component, which will further guarantee that when the selected typeface is realized

Hutchins Center for African & African American Research
Bruce Mau Design
Toronto, ON, CA
This visual identity system is comprised of two type-based elements, a bold Sans Serif Grotesque symbol and a bold, upper and lowercase Old Style serif logotype which function equally and with the same visual integrity in both print-based and low-resolution, digital-based applications.

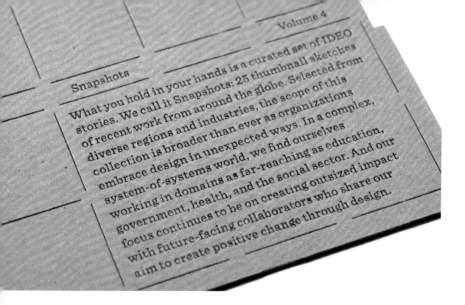

IDEO Snapshots Series
Volume Inc.
San Francisco, CA, USA
**This self-promotional
series relies upon a
tactile material solution
so that the visual integ-
rity of all Slab Serif type,
Sentinel (Jonathan
Hoefler, Tobias Frere-
Jones, 2009), could be
maintained. Materials
and processes include
black foil stamping on
die-cut chipboard, digital
printing on uncoated
card stock, and printed
elastic bands.**

in a traditional medium such as print, or
in digital media such as a website, the
selection will function equally and with the
same visual integrity.

Print Applications
When selecting a particular typeface for
printing on paper or other porous substrates,
you need to understand the specifications of
the surface the type is to be printed on, which
could impact the final resolution and printing
of that typeface. For example, if the paper
surface is uncoated and has a woven finish
(which is more absorbent to ink), a small-scale
text setting of Bodoni (Giambattista Bodoni,
1798; see page 35), a Modern serif typeface,
may not hold up as well in printing compared
to Univers (Adrian Frutiger, 1976), a San Serif
Neo-Grotesque typeface, due to their extreme
stroke and terminal variations.

A graphic designer needs to remember
that different papers and porous substrates
have a broad range of characteristics and
properties that need to be taken into account

prior to selecting a typeface. The integrity of any typeface will be affected by printing methods such as offset, digital, letterpress, thermography, engraving, silk-screening, embossing, and debossing.

The more you understand about the performance specifications of the print medium being used, the more successful the typographic end result will be.

Pairing Typefaces

While there are no definitive rules that you need to follow when it comes to pairing type-faces, it is clear that most readers can engage with two fonts, possibly three, but never more than that. A primary rule in this context is also contrast. For example, when pairing two or more San Serif Neo-Grotesque typefaces, such as Helvetica (Max Miedinger, 1956; see page 51) and Univers (Adrian Frutiger, 1976), or Slab Serif typefaces, such as Clarendon (Robert Besley, 1845; see page 40) and Archer (Jonathan Hoefler, 2001; see page 43), that possess similar visual characteristics, a reader will be confused and lose patience due to lack of clarity and intent, whereas an obvious and visible distinction between two or more typefaces paired will always have an appeal and ease for most readers.

As an alternative to pairing two or more distinct and unique typefaces, many type foundries today design typeface families that offer an extensive range of weights, widths, styles, and character sets that provide graphic designers with a multitude of options for creating visual emphasis and hierarchy. Visual distinction and appropriateness need to be carefully considered when using more than one typeface within any text setting.

Method + Standard
Device Creative Collaborative
Winston-Salem, NC, USA
This bold and distinctive brand identity and pack-aging relies upon the pairing of two different typefaces from two distinct type classifica-tions, Modern and Sans Serif Geometric—Craw Modern (Freeman Craw, 1958) and Gotham (Tobias Frere-Jones, 2000), and presents the brand typography reading in both orienta-tions, offering different visual experiences when viewing and pouring.

Midnight Moon
Device Creative
Collaborative
Winston-Salem, NC, USA
**Three distinct typefaces
from three different
type classifications,
Sans Serif Grotesque,
Script, and Decorative,
are paired for this brand
identity and packag-
ing of a triple-distilled,
lower-proof and legal
version of Moonshine.
These traditional and
handwritten letterforms
allude to a generations-
back approach to
Prohibition-era distilling.**

For example, the inherent contrast between serif and Sans Serif typefaces may be more visually effective and immediate than using two serif or Sans Serif typefaces together.

Whether relying upon two or more different typefaces or one extensive typeface family with varying weights and styles, graphic designers have a broad range of typographic form options to select from when considering typefaces for their work. These varied options enable you to achieve, and ultimately communicate organization, hierarchy, and differentiation to a reader with varied content while still maintaining a visual harmony in the end result.

Test your Knowledge

1. What are three (3) critical considerations when evaluating a typeface for selection?

2. What are three (3) important factors for a graphic designer to consider relating to audience when evaluating a typeface for selection?

3. What visual characteristics and physical attributes of typefaces make them more compatible with one another?

4. What are three (3) text-based type-faces and their type classifications which are primarily used for continuous and uninterrupted reading in book-scale applications?

5. Name three (3) display-based typefaces.

6. Name three (3) typographic principles of measurement and spacing that affect readability and legibility in type selection.

7. Name four (4) type characteristics that need to be considered when evaluating and ultimately selecting a typeface for text settings.

8. Identify the modernist American architect who is known for the design credo "form follows function."

9. Identify two (2) visual and physical characteristics of a typeface that need to be considered when evaluating and selecting a typeface.

For answers to Test your Knowledge, see page 230.

Section 6

Typography in Practice

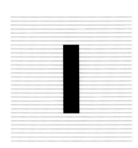n everyday occurrences and interactions, we hear someone say that they have "expressed their opinion." However, visual expression or communications is something more concrete, more specific, more objective, and more intentional. Meaningful and memorable graphic design occurs when its fundamental elements and principles, such as type, are used selectively and collectively by a graphic designer to create a "visual experience" for the reader.

Expression is a design principle fully dependent on your own creativity, imagination, individual ideas, personal moods, sole emotional outlook on the world, and place within it. It is perceived visually, as well as psychologically, in any visual message. It is a completely subjective principle and reflects directly on the time and experiences in which you have lived. Expression cannot be taught; it is learned by each and every graphic designer. It is also a reflection of your inner thoughts, dreams, fears, and passions. As a result, an inherent bias completely depends upon separate experiences or realities that ultimately influence your own creative process, choices, and work.

Since the beginning of human development, we have had the desire, as well as the basic need, to express ourselves. While graphic design as a discipline has had a relatively short history, with the term "graphic design" first coined by renowned type designer, calligrapher, and book designer William Addison Dwiggins (American, 1880–1956) in 1922, visual communications, including type, have always been an integral part of our human history. It is evident in the prehistoric cave paintings of northern Spain and southern France (ca. 15000 BCE), the Roman Forum's Trajan Column (ca. 113 CE), the illuminated medieval manuscripts and incunabula of the Middle Ages (ca. 600–1600 CE), and in the mesmerizing neon signs of Times Square (ca. 1904) and Piccadilly Circus (ca. 1923).

Graphic design provides a means for you to "express" your own imagination in ways that do not rely solely upon spoken or written language. Every element used in graphic design, such as type, has the potential to express something specific. Although the explanation and ultimate use of design

elements and principles may seem cut-and-dry, the quality of these elements and principles is perceived solely through the expression of the total message by a graphic designer.

Type is one of the most powerful forms of visual expression and communications. When used in combination with imagery, color, and other relevant design elements, it can convey a memorable and timeless message that will always be associated with a specific human emotion.

Typography is the process of arranging letters, words, and text for any context, and it is among the most important design principles for creating effective and meaningful graphic design. You learn the nuances of type in order to use it creatively, while maintaining respect for its rules and traditions.

This section not only explores the student experience; it includes work by some of the most successful and renowned practitioners from around the world, examining how they have applied these fundamental principles of type to their work. By examining this work, *Design School: Type* is also a more meaningful, memorable, and inspiring reference for students, as well as for novice practitioners starting their professional careers.

The following pages provide visual references you can fully embrace, as well as being a catalyst for exploring new concepts, technologies, materials, and styles with confidence and assurance. Hopefully, this work will also help you achieve a greater power and influence in your craft and discipline—a power to inform, educate, and/or persuade a single person or collective audience in a meaningful and memorable way—with type.

Type Classifications
Humanist, Old Style

Carlo Dolci and
17th-Century Florence
Stoltze Design
Boston, MA, USA
A calligraphic influence
is evident in a Humanist
serif typeface used
for this exhibition
catalog cover since
it possesses minimal
contrast between thick
and thin strokes and a
strong inclined stress,
reflecting earlier
letterforms drawn with
a broad-nibbed pen.

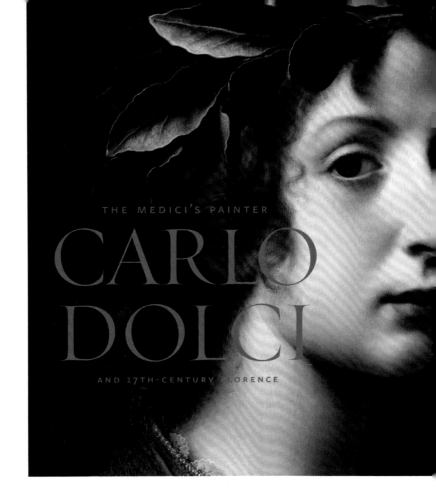

THE MEDICI'S PAINTER

CARLO
DOLCI

AND 17TH-CENTURY FLORENCE

Hutchins Center
for African &
African American
Research

Harvard
Univ

Hutchins Center
for African & African
American Research
Bruce Mau Design
Toronto, ON, CA
The Hutchins Center
for African & African
American Research at
Harvard University
houses a group of
world-leading research
institutes and pro-
grams dedicated to
the creation of cutting-
edge knowledge in the
field of African and
African American
research. Their new
visual identity system
is comprised of two
type-based elements, a
bold Sans Serif symbol
and a bold, upper and
lowercase Old Style serif
logotype that function
equally and with the
same visual integrity
in both print-based and
low-resolution, digital-
based applications.

Transitional, Modern, Slab Serif

**Charlotte Brooks
at Look: 1951–1971**
Stoltze Design
Boston, MA, USA
**A pronounced contrast
of thinner strokes,
appearing as a hairline
weight, with thick and
exaggerated heavier
strokes, in comparison
emphasizing vertical
stress, is a prominent
visual characteristic of
a Modern serif typeface
used for this exhibition
catalog cover.**

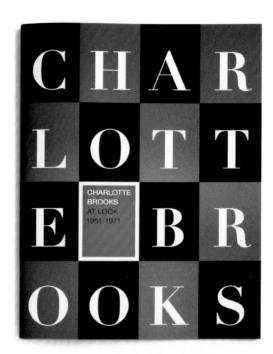

Devona
Hinterland
New York, NY, USA
**An interactive agency's
brand Identity utilizes
a custom, monotone
Slab Serif typeface with
short, unbracketed
serifs that takes its
visual cues from binary
code and information
data exchange.**

LESLIE WILLIAMSON

Modern Originals
Volume Inc.
San Francisco, CA, USA
**Modern Originals, a
Eurocentric sequel
to the popular
Handcrafted Modern
book series, show-
cases the workplaces
of famous architects and
designers and effectively
uses an unconventional
Modern stenciled-serif
typeface, Danmark
(Henrik Kubel, 2008)
for large-scale titling
and drop caps.**

Sans Serif (Grotesque, Neo-Grotesque, Geometric, Humanist)

Coachmen Electric
Jiwon Chong (Student),
Scott Buschkuhl
(Instructor)
School of Visual Arts
New York, NY, USA
A Sans Serif Geometric typeface, Brown (Aurèle Sack, 2011), provides a typographic opportunity for creating a dual identity for E and T, as well as glyphs for polarity symbols.

Swissted
Stereotype Design
New York, NY, USA
This is a poster series of vintage punk, hardcore, new wave, and indie rock shows that have been reimagined in the Swiss Style genre with all typographic elements set in lowercase Akzidenz Grotesk (1896), a Sans Serif Neo-Grotesque typeface.

DNE India
Hinterland
New York, NY, USA
This book celebrates the various connections between the peoples of Northeast India and reflects a poetic use of language, color, scale, and type with the use of a Sans Serif Geometric typeface, Priori Sans (Jonathan Barnbrook, Marcus Leis Allion, 2003), and a Casual Script typeface, Notera (Måns Grebäck, 2014).

Papier 14 and 15
Jolin Masson
Montréal, QC, CA
This visual identity communicates a modern and accessible brand by using a Sans Serif Humanist typeface, Open Sans, (Steve Matteson, 2010), for all primary type elements with a contemporary Old Style serif typeface, Mercury Text (Jonathan Hoefler, Tobias Frere-Jones, 1999) for all narrative text and caption information.

Type Classifications
Glyphic, Script, Decorative

Maël
Lorenzo Geiger
Bern, Zurich, CH
Distinctive triangular-shaped serifs and sharp, flared terminals of this Glyphic display typeface's character strokes add a spirited visual nuance to this CD cover for Maël's *Feels Like Christmas*.

Martin Luther King, Jr.
Alexander Catanese
(Student), Jillian Coorey
(Instructor)
Kent State University
Kent, OH, USA
A spontaneous and dramatic, hand-drawn appearance of these Casual Script letterforms appearing throughout this book on Martin Luther King Jr. conveys a visual energy and sound-like experience that is evocative of the power and import of his words.

Ana Pro
Vedran Erakovic
Belgrade, RS

Ana Pro is an auto-chromatic typeface consisting of uppercase Latin characters, inspired by arabesque patterns from the nineteenth century. Programmed to enable users to easily create multicolored drop caps and initials, this Decorative display typeface features a different ornament for every letterform, which fits perfectly with its glyph shape.

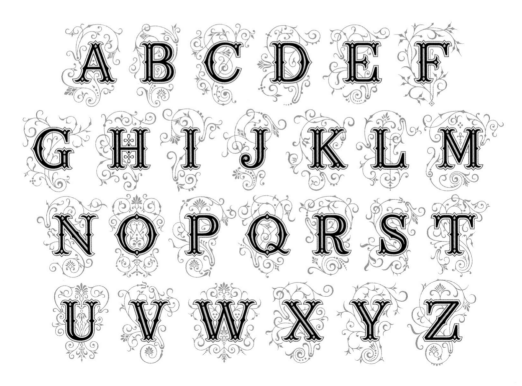

Lucky Penny
Frost* Collective
Sydney, NSW, AUS
Using an adaptation of a Decorative display typeface, India (Henrik Kubel, 2011), this three-dimensional typographic installation of copper piping communicates a brand gesture of "luck" for the history of a building when it was tenanted by a luxury women's handbag company.

Street Sweets
Landers Miller Design
Portland, OR, USA
Cyclone (Jonathan Hoefler, 2000) is a Decorative inline display typeface used in a dense arrangement of verbs and adjectives that create an active pattern for this dessert food truck identity and branding program.

The Essential

Goethe

JOHANN WOLFGANG VON GOETHE

Edited and Introduced by

MATTHEW BELL

PRINCETON UNIVERSITY PRESS
Princeton & Oxford

On Literature and Art

ON GERMAN ARCHITECTURE
(1772)

On a pilgrimage to your grave, noble Erwin, I searched for the tombstone with the inscription, *Anno Domini 1318. XVI Kal. Febr. Obiit Magister Ervinus, Gubernator Fabricae Ecclesiae Argentinensis*. But I could not find it, nor were any of your countrymen able to help me. And I was saddened to the depth of my soul, for I had come to pour out my veneration for you at that hallowed place. My heart, younger then, warmer, more foolish and better than now, solemnly vowed that once in due possession of my inheritance, I would build you a memorial of marble or of sandstone, whichever I could afford.

Yet you need no memorial! You erected your own, a magnificent one. And though the throngs crawling about it like ants know nothing of your name, you are like the Great Architect who piled up mountains into the clouds.

Few have been blessed with a mind capable of conceiving a Babel-like vision—whole, great, inherently beautiful to the last detail, like God's trees—and even fewer with the good fortune to encounter a thousand willing hands, to excavate the rocky foundations, to conjure up towering structures and, with their dying breath, tell their sons: I will remain with you in the works of my spirit. Complete what is begun, until it reaches into the clouds.

You need no memorial! Certainly not mine! When the rabble utter sacred names, it is superstition or blasphemy. The feeble esthete will feel forever giddy in the presence of your colossus, robust sensibilities will understand you without an interpreter.

Now then, worthy Erwin, before I venture back to sea in my fragile bark, more likely to encounter death than prosperity, behold this grove where I engraved the names of beloved friends, there I will cut yours into a beech tree slender and soaring like your tower, and in its branches I will hang by its four corners this handkerchief full of gifts. It resembles the sheet that was let down from the clouds to the holy apostle, full of clean and unclean beasts. So mine will be filled with flowers, blossoms, leaves, but also dry grass and moss and toadstools sprung up over night—everything I gathered while walking

867

The Essential Goethe
Chris Ferrante
Princeton, NJ, USA
An over-scaled, bold typographic treatment for this book jacket clearly conveys a historical accuracy and relevance to the book's subject matter by utilizing Blackletter or Textura. Secondary italic and all-cap serif letterforms organized symmetrically on the cover and interior pages further reinforce the historical context of the book's time period and theme.

Terminology
Type Anatomy, Serif Anatomy, Terminal Anatomy

The Forgotten Windows
Krishnapriya Datta
(Student), Kathrin Blatter
(Instructor)
Academy of Art
University
San Francisco, CA, USA
Posters for an architectural lecture series explore classic windows across geography and history by effectively relying upon the even stroke thickness of a Sans Serif Grotesque typeface, Poster Gothic (Morris Fuller Benton, 1934; Mark van Bronkhorst, Luis Batlle, Igino Marini, Ben Kiel, 2015), to three-dimensionalize each window's visual effect in a unified manner.

Hummingbird
Leona Legarte (Student),
California College of
the Arts
San Francisco, CA, USA
Acute, tapered terminals of this logotype's custom typeface are an obvious extension of the brand's symbol and further communicate movement and bird-like visual characteristics.

214

Black Pine
Device Creative
Collaborative
Winston-Salem, NC, USA
**Ornamental letterforms,
serifs, and terminals
of a Decorative display
typeface, LHF Firehouse
(Thomas Kennedy,
2004), are evocative
of Victorian hand-carved
signs and maker's
marks, and function as
the primary typographic
logotype for this real
estate firm.**

introducing

chimera

a technologically enhanced
typeface for the coming
transhuman age

contextual alternates

part human
part animal
part machine

Chimera
Margaret Andersen
(Student), Rachel Berger
(Instructor)
California College of
the Arts
Valencia, CA, USA
**This custom typeface
was designed to
accompany a student
MFA thesis on
bioengineering and
genomic research and
is a hybrid font created
by combining different
type anatomy, serifs,
terminals, and
glyphs from Modern
serif-based typefaces.**

**The Market
@ Novo Nordisk**
Poulin + Morris Inc.
New York, NY, USA
**Knockout (Jonthan
Hoefler, Tobias Frere-
Jones, 1990), an
extensive Sans Serif
Grotesque type family
of 32 weight and width
variations, was used
for this self-service
"grab and go" branding
program to convey
a fun, energetic, and
non-corporate visual
experience in an
otherwise rigorous
corporate headquarters
environment.**

Capco
Bruce Mau Design
Toronto, ON, CA
**This brand identity is
built on "structured
flexibility," a key tenet
of this international
financial consultancy,
where the Sans Serif
Grotesque wordmark
is bold and stable, while
the dynamic "C," or
bracket, can easily frame
different messages
through text or imagery.**

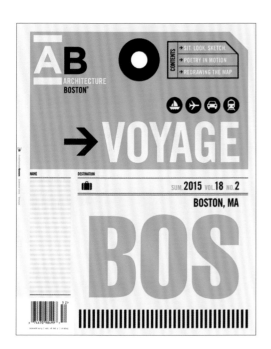

Architecture Boston
Stoltze Design
Boston, MA, USA
This cover is representative of the extensive variations in typographic forms found in the Sans Serif Grotesque typeface used for this quarterly magazine. A diverse set of type styles, weights, and glyphs adds visual nuance in a unified and integrated manner.

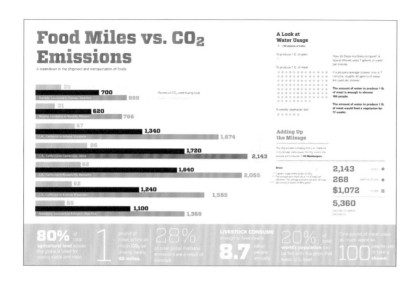

**Fork in the Road, A
Meaty Issue, Food Miles
vs. CO2 Emissions**
Gina LaRocca (Student)
Jillian Coorey (Instructor)
Kent State University
Kent, OH, USA
**This editorial spread
shows the effective
use of a Slab Serif
typeface in a variety of
compositional contexts,
from narrative text to
informational and
statistical data; each
spaced and placed within
optimum line measures.**

**SFMoMa Film and Public
Programs: Jeff Wall**
MendeDesign
San Francisco, CA, USA
**This poster is part of an
ongoing series, each with
a unique visual language
and composition to com-
municate the curatorial
vision behind each pro-
gram. In this example, a
measured square-based
grid with square-based
letterforms is used.**

**MSG Media
Headquarters**
Poulin + Morris Inc.
New York, NY, USA
**Layered, varied-sized
and -spaced quotes
from fans, players,
and news media set
in a Sans Serif Grotesque
typeface, Tungsten
(Jonathan Hoefler,
Tobias Frere-Jones,
2009), function as a
continuous typographic
narrative for a series of
iconic moments that
commemorate Madison
Square Garden Media's
influence and impact
on the public realm.**

**McGill School of
Architecture
Final Reviews**
Atelier Pastille Rose
Montréal, QC, CA
**The organization
and symmetrical
composition of this
announcement
poster is based on a
thorough understand-
ing of columnar or
line measure and
typographic spacing,
leading, kerning,
and letter spacing.**

Typographic Principles
Alignment

Mural at Present 2009

Nakamura
Keith Haring Collection
Hinterland
New York, NY, USA

This dual language book investigates the connections between Keith Haring and Japanese culture by employing minimalist typography organized in a columnar grid with two alignment formats—flush left for English, justified for Japanese. English is a Sans Serif Geometric typeface, Gotham Rounded (Tobias Frere-Jones, 2005), and Japanese is a Sans Serif Grotesque typeface, HC Maru Gothic.

220

**McGill School of
Architecture
Final Reviews**
Atelier Pastille Rose
Montréal, QC, CA
**This poster series relies
on a flush left alignment
for both sizes of
typographic information.
This apparent visual
difference due to their
extreme sizes allows
the reader to experience
both scales separately
and easily.**

**Barclay Simpson MFA
Exhibition**
Phillip Barnard (Student),
Rachel Berger (Instructor)
California College of
the Arts
San Francisco, CA, USA
**The centered alignment
of this poster for an MFA
thesis exhibition
provides a compositional
and organizational
structure for both sizes
of Sans Serif typographic
information—a large-
scale exhibition title with
a small-scale listing of
participant names.**

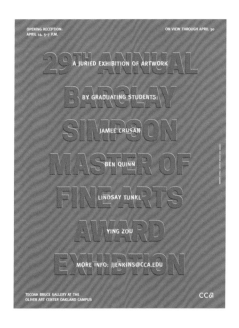

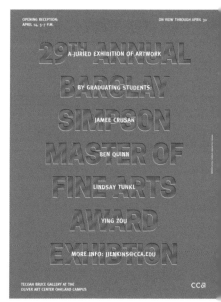

Readability and Legibility, Emphasis and Hierarchy

Vitium
Fay Change (Student),
Rachel Berger (Instructor)
California College of
the Arts
San Francisco, CA, USA
**Emphasis and hierarchy
are used effectively
with this larger-scale,
all-cap Sans Serif
logotype contrasted
with a smaller-scale,
lowercase serif italic
descriptive line centered
directly below.**

*Gibney Dance
Community Action*
Poulin + Morris Inc.
New York, NY, USA
**Dramatic typographic
scale and orientations
in a Sans Serif
Geometric typeface,
Flama Condensed
(Mário Felciano, 2008),
are coupled with
bold and vibrant color
to emphasize visual
data and narrative
information on this
community-based
program that teaches
survivors of domestic
violence methods of
self-expression through
dance and movement.**

Blueprint

Paolo Cockriel (Student),
Adrian Pulfer (Instructor)
Brigham Young University
Washington, DC, USA

These editorial spreads reflect optimum readability, legibility, emphasis, and hierarchy by relying upon a singular Sans Serif Neo-Grotesque typeface used throughout and composed in a variety of weights, styles, and orientation formats.

Frui De Mer Boeri In Marseille: What the team thinks you've ever wondered about this this place.All you've ever wondered about this place.

Milan Review: All you've ever wondered about this this place.All you've ever wondered about this place.

Frui De Mer Boeri In Marseille: What the team thinks you've ever wondered about this this place.

Milan Review: All you've ever wondered about this this place.All you've ever wondered about this place.

Rijks Museum Revamp: Again with the Obscure other smudges titles.

022 RIJKS MUSEUM REVAMP

045 FRUI DE MER BOERI IN MARSEILLE

079 MILAN REVIEW

016

For the architects it has been an important investigation into both temporary structures –

THE SHED
NEW YORK / JOEL NEWMAN

Sed ut perspiciatis unde omnis iste natus error sit voluptatem accusantium doloremque laudantium, Nemo enim ipsam voluptatem quia voluptas sit aspernatur aut odit aut fugit, sed quia consequuntur magni dolores eos qui ratione.

Nequi nesciunt. Neque porro quisquam est, qui dolorem ipsum quia dolor sit amet, consectetur, adipisci velit, sed quia non numquam eius modi tempora incidunt ut labore et dolore magnam aliquam quaerat voluptatem. Ut enim ad minima veniam, quis nostrum exercitationem ullam corporis suscipit laboriosam, nisi ut aliquid ex ea commodi consequatur? Quis autem vel eum iure reprehenderit qui in ea voluptate velit esse quam nihil molestiae consequatur, vel illum qui dolorem eum fugiat quo voluptas nulla pariatur?"

Neque porro quisquam est, qui dolorem ipsum quia dolor sit amet, consectetur, adipisci velit, sed quia non numquam eius modi tempora incidunt ut labore et dolore magnam aliquam quaerat voluptatem. Ut enim ad minima veniam, quis nostrum exercitationem ullam corporis suscipit laboriosam, nisi ut aliquid ex ea commodi consequatur? Quis autem vel eum iure reprehenderit qui in ea voluptate velit esse quam nihil molestiae consequatur, vel illum qui dolorem eum fugiat quo voluptas nulla pariatur?"Neque porro quisquam est, qui dolorem ipsum quia dolor sit amet, consectetur, adipisci velit, sed quia non numquam eius modi tempora incidunt ut labore et dolore magnam aliquam quaerat voluptatem. Ut enim ad minima veniam, quis nostrum exercitationem ullam corporis suscipit laboriosam, nisi ut aliquid ex ea commodi consequatur? Quis autem vel eum iure reprehenderit qui in ea voluptate velit esse quam nihil molestiae consequatur, vel illum qui dolorem eum fugiat quo voluptas nulla pariatur?"

Sed ut perspiciatis unde omnis iste natus error sit voluptatem accusantium doloremque laudantium, Nemo enim ipsam voluptatem quia voluptas sit aspernatur aut odit aut fugit, sed quia consequuntur magni dolores eos qui ratione.

nequi nesciunt. Neque porro quisquam est, qui dolorem ipsum quia dolor sit amet, consectetur, adipisci velit, sed quia non numquam eius modi tempora incidunt ut labore et dolore magnam aliquam quaerat voluptatem. Ut enim ad minima veniam, quis nostrum exercitationem ullam corporis suscipit laboriosam, nisi ut aliquid ex ea commodi consequatur? Quis autem vel eum iure reprehenderit qui in ea voluptate velit esse quam nihil molestiae consequatur, vel illum qui dolorem eum fugiat quo voluptas nulla pariatur?"

Neque porro quisquam est, qui dolorem ipsum quia dolor sit amet, consectetur, adipisci velit, sed quia non numquam eius modi tempora incidunt ut labore et dolore magnam aliquam quaerat voluptatem. Ut enim ad minima veniam, quis nostrum exercitationem ullam corporis suscipit laboriosam, nisi ut aliquid ex ea commodi

Sed ut perspiciatis unde omnis iste natus sollicitated sit volus adfled platenut accusanadf itam adfed adfed fadfed dolorempurself

– and new forms of theatre.

Jewish Museum

Jewish Museum
Sagmeister & Walsh
New York, NY, USA
This rebranding program's context is based on "sacred geometry," an ancient geometric system from which the Star of David was formed, with all program elements drawn from this grid, from its custom wordmark and logotype to patterns, icons, typography, and illustrations. The program invites surprise and flexibility across all print and digital media, while being unified in its visual language.

Sasaki
Bruce Mau Design
Toronto, ON, CA
This identity system for Sasaki, a global planning and design practice, is comprised of a word-mark generated from four geometric shapes that shift in color to create vibrant logotype variations. These shapes are then used to form patterns, visual language elements, and a custom Sans Serif display typeface.

Well Rounded Sound
Hinterland
New York, NY, USA
Inspired by sound waves, as well as the shape of their audio speakers, a Sans Serif Geometric typeface, Gotham Rounded (Tobias Frere-Jones, 2005), was used as the context for this audiophile equipment manufacturer's logotype, and paired with a stylized acronym-based symbol.

Selecting Typefaces
For Visual Harmony

Constitution Wharf
Poulin + Morris Inc.
New York, NY, USA
**This logotype is a
Sans Serif Geometric
typeface, Flama
Ultra-Condensed (Mário
Feliciano, 2004), and
a Slab Serif typeface,
Produkt (Berton Hasebe,
Christian Schwartz,
2014), conveying its
duality as a twenty-first
century commercial
office complex in a
historic location.**

L'Observatoire
Triboro
New York, NY, USA
**The interplay of light
and shadow is the
primary graphic theme
of this identity program
for a lighting design
studio and relies on the
fine line stroke and
pure geometry of a Sans
Serif Geometric
typeface, Larsseit (Nico
Inosanto, 2013).**

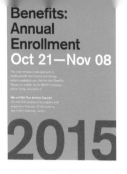

Credit Suisse
Carbone Smolan Agency
New York, NY, USA
This extensive branding system and global recruiting campaign for a financial services and wealth management firm, ranging from poster templates to standardized iconography and data visualization design standards, relies upon a vivid color palette, striking photographic images, rigorous page grids, asymmetrical compositional layouts, and Sans Serif Neo-Grotesque typography. Akzidenz Grotesk (1896), a typeface favored by typographers and graphic designers of the Swiss International Typographic Style. It is an appropriate and relevant type choice for this modern context and is used consistently throughout the campaign's print and digital applications.

Test your Knowledge Answers

Section 1: Type Classifications

1. The Humanist type classification marks the start of the refinement of typographic form from centuries of handwritten and calligraphic-based letterforms to a more articulated and delineated type genre.

2. Garalde is another identifier for Old Style type classification.

3. The Old Style type classification includes the typefaces Bembo, Garamond, and Goudy.

4. The primary visual characteristics of Transitional typefaces are geometric rather than hand-drawn forms, vertical stress in curved letterforms, sharper bracketed serifs, pronounced contrast in stroke thickness, and large x-heights.

5. The following fonts are not Transitional typefaces: (a) Bembo (b) Bodoni (d) Melior and (e) Sabon.

6. The Modern type classification was highly influenced by the typefaces designed by Giambattista Bodoni and Firmin Didot.

7. The primary visual characteristics of Modern typefaces are extreme and abrupt contrast in stroke weights, thin and completely flat serifs, almost invariably vertical stress axis with little or no bracketing, and letterform with very tight apertures.

8. The Slab Serif type classification is used to identify the first display typefaces specifically designed for large-scale display needs.

9. Four (4) subcategories of the Sans Serif type classification are Grotesque, Neo-Grotesque, Geometric, and Humanist.

10. The primary visual characteristics of Glyphic typefaces are minimal contrast in stroke widths, a vertical stress axis for most curved stroke letterforms, and triangular-shaped serif or sharp, flared terminals.

11. Chancery is the term used to identify the first script-based typefaces which were produced in Italy at the end of the fifteenth century.

12. Three (3) subcategories of the Script type classification are Formal, Casual, and Calligraphic.

13. The Decorative type classification includes ornamental, specialty, and novelty typefaces.

14. Four (4) separate and distinct subcategories of the Blackletter type classification are Textura, Bastarda (or Schwabacher), Fraktur, and Rotunda.

Section 2: Terminology

1. The outer point of a letterform where two diagonal stems or strokes meet, such as at the highest point of an A or M or at the bottom of an M, is called an apex.

2. The area that is either fully or partially enclosed by a bowl or a cross bar of a letterform, as in a b, p, o, or A is called a counter.

3. The two letterforms found in many typefaces that can be either single- or double-story are an a and g.

4. The adjustable vertical space that is located between lines of type, and specified as a measurement in points from baseline to baseline, is called leading.

5. Other names for a minuscule and majuscule are lowercase and uppercase.

6. Three (3) primary visual characteristics of Old Style typefaces are low contrast between thick and thin strokes, a left-leaning axis or stress, and bracketed serifs.

7. Three (3) primary visual characteristics of Transitional typefaces are a subtle contrast between thick and thin strokes, minimal left-inclined stress, and a triangular or flat tip where diagonal strokes meet, such as at the base of a W.

8. Two (2) primary visual characteristics of Modern typefaces are an extreme contrast between thick and thin strokes, as well as flat serifs.

9. The measured distance from the baseline to the top of the lowercase x is called x-height.

10. A single word or line of text at the beginning of a paragraph located at the bottom of a page or column of text is called a widow.

11. Two (2) typefaces that have unbracketed serifs are Didot (Firmin Didot, 1799) and Bodoni (Giambattista Bodoni, 1798).

12. The inclination of thin and thick, curved stems or strokes in a letterform is called vertical stress or axis.

13. Antique, Egyptian, Egyptienne, and Square Serif are other names for the Slab Serif type classification.

14. Calligraphic, Casual, and Formal are other names for the Script type classification.

15. "SCOSF" means small capitals and old style figures.

16. A noticeable gap of white space running vertically through a column of text is called a river.

17. The smallest typographic unit of measurement is a point, which equals 0.0139 inches (0.0353 cm).

18. A single word or line of text at the end of a paragraph located at the top of a page or column of text is called an orphan.

Section 3: Characters and Glyphs

1. The main visual characteristics of lining figures is a fixed height that matches the height of capitals or uppercase letterforms and that they always sit on a baseline.

2. The main visual characteristics of old style figures is a variable-height that matches the same proportions and profiles of lowercase letterforms, and that they align to the x-height rather than the cap height of a typeface, and have ascending and descending strokes.

3. The typeface and its type classification that Adrian Frutiger (Swiss, 1928–2015) designed and organized on the premise of a "periodic table" is called Univers (1954), a Sans Serif Neo-Grotesque.

4. The typographic glyph composed of a group of characters that follows a figure or number to indicate sequence or position, such as 1st, 2nd, or 3rd, is called an ordinal indicator.

5. The glyph that is added to a letterform to indicate a change or variation in the pronunciation or sound of that letter or word is called a diacritical mark.

6. The typographic glyph used in place of the word "and," and derived from the ligature for the Latin word "et," is called an ampersand.

7. The punctuation glyph comprised of three evenly spaced dots or periods in a row and indicating a missing word or phrase, is called an ellipsis.

8. Two of the most popular non-typographic dingbat font sets available today are Hermann Zapf's Zapf Dingbats (1978) and Zuzana Licko's Whirligig (1994).

9. The primary function of an initial letter, drop cap, or initial cap in any text setting is to indicate the first character of a text paragraph, as well as the start of a new section within running text, such as a chapter.

Test your Knowledge Answers continued

Section 4: Typographic Principles

1. Two (2) standard units of measurement that the American–British Point System are based on are point and pica.

2. The unit of measurement that is derived from the width of a square body of the cast uppercase "M" is called an em.

3. Adjustable space located between letters is called letter spacing or tracking.

4. Adjustment of horizontal space located between one or more pairs of individual characters is called kerning.

5. Adjustable vertical space located between lines of type is called leading.

6. Four (4) basic compositional alignment formats that provide options for the organization and positioning of typographic lines of continuous text are flush left, flush right, justified, and centered.

7. An uneven textural edge created by varied lengths of text lines is called a rag.

8. The common measurement of x-height can be to visually unify two or more distinct typefaces when they share a common baseline in any continuous text setting.

9. Four (4) main factors that influence the readability of any text setting are line length or measure, character count per line, spacing, and case.

10 Three (3) visual cues to reinforce visual hierarchy and organization in any text setting are indents, line spacing, and type style and weight variations.

Section 5: Selecting Typefaces

1. Three (3) critical considerations when evaluating a typeface for selection are history, classification, and formal visual characteristics.

2. Three (3) important factors to consider relating to audience when evaluating a typeface for selection are content, context, and meaning.

3. The visual characteristics and physical attributes of typefaces that make them more compatible with one another are proportions, stroke weights, x-heights, and cap heights.

4. Three (3) text-based typefaces and their type classifications primarily used for continuous and uninterrupted reading in book-scale applications are Jenson (Nicolas Jenson, 1471) Humanist; Garamond (Claude Garamond, ca. 1530) Old Style; and Baskerville (John Baskerville, 1757) Transitional.

5. Three (3) display-based typefaces are Broadway (Morris Fuller Benton, 1929), Entropy (Stephen Farrell, 1993), and Sophia (Matthew Carter, 1993).

6. Three (3) typographic principles of measurement and spacing that effect readability and legibility in type selection are line length or measure, character count per line, and leading.

7. Four (4) type characteristics that need to be considered when evaluating and ultimately selecting a typeface for text settings are larger x-heights, counters, ascenders and descenders, and double-story lowercase letterforms (a or g).

8. The modernist American architect who is known for the design credo "form follows function" is Louis Sullivan.

9. Two (2) visual and physical characteristics of a typeface that need to be considered when evaluating and selecting a typeface are size and line spacing.

Resources

Typographic Organizations

American Institute of Graphic Arts
aiga.org

Association Typographique Internationale (ATypl)
atypi.org

International Council of Graphic Design Associations (ICOGRADA)
icograda.org

International Society of Typographic Designers
istd.org.uk

Type Directors Club (TDC)
tdc.org

Online Typographic Resources

Beautiful Type
beautifultype.com

The Font Feed
fontfeed.com

Fonts In Use
fontsinuse.com

I Love Typography
ilovetypography.com

Lettercult
lettercult.com

Microsoft Typography
microsoft.com/typography/

TypeCulture
typeculture.com

Typedia
typedia.com

Typewolf
Typewolf.com

Typophile
typophile.com

We Love Typography
welovetypography.com

Type Foundries and Type Designers

Adobe Systems Incorporated
adobe.com/type

A-Type
a2-type.co.uk

H. Berthold AG
bertholdtypes.com

Bitstream Inc.
bitstream.com

Commercial Type
commercialtype.com

Dalton Maag
daltonmaag.com

Darden Studio
dardenstudio.com

Dutch Type Library
dutchtypelibrary.nl

Émigré
emigre.com

The Font Bureau
fontbureau.com

FontFont
fontfont.com

FontHaus
fonthaus.com

Font Shop
fontshop.com

Frere-Jones Type
frerejones.com

Grilli Type
grillitype.com

Gerard Unger
gerardunger.com

Hoefler & Co.
typography.com

House Industries
houseind.com

International Typeface Corporation
itcfonts.com

Klim Type Foundry
klim.co.nz

Kent Lew
kentlew.com

Linotype
linotype.com

Lucas Fonts
lucasfonts.com

Monotype Imaging
monotypeimaging.com

P22 Type Foundry
p22.com

Parachute Fonts
parachutefonts.com

Process Type Foundry
processtypefoundry.com

Mark Simonson
marksimonson.com

Sudtipos
sudtipos.com

T26
t26.com

Thirstype
thirstype.com

TypeTogether
type-togther.com

Typofonderie
typofonderie.com

Typotheque
typotheque.com

Underware Type Foundry
underware.nl

Village
vllg.com

Virus Fonts
virusfonts.com

Bibliography

Ambrose, Gavin and Harris, Paul. *Typography*. Lausanne: AVA Publishing SA, 2005.

Ambrose, Gavin and Harris, Paul. *The Fundamentals of Typography*. Lausanne: AVA Publishing SA, 2007.

Arntson, Amy E. *Graphic Design Basics*, New York: Rinehart and Winston, 1988.

Ball, Johnson. *William Caslon: Master of Letters*. Warwick: The Roundwood Press, 1973.

Blackwell, Lewis. *20th Century Type*. New York: Rizzoli International Publications, Inc., 2004.

Bringhurst, Robert. *The Elements of Typographic Style, Version 3.1*. Vancouver: Hartley and Marks, 2005.

Burke, Christopher. *Paul Renner: The Art of Typography*. New York: Princeton Architectural Press, 1998.

Carter, Rob; Day, Ben; and Meggs, Philip. *Typographic Design: Form and Communication*. New York: Van Nostrand Reinhold, 1993.

Chappell, Warren; Bringhurst, Robert. *A Short History of the Printed Word*. Vancouver: Hartley & Marks Publishers, 2000.

Cheng, Karen. *Designing Type*. New Haven: Yale University Press, 2006.

Cohen, Arthur A. *Herbert Bayer: The Complete Work*. Cambridge: MIT Press, 1984.

Coles, Stephen. *The Anatomy of Type: A Graphic Guide to 100 Typefaces*. New York: Harper Design, 2012.

Dabner, David; Stewart, Sandra; and Zempol, Eric. *Graphic Design School: The Principles and Practice of Graphic Design*. Hoboken: John Wiley & Sons, 2014.

De Jong, Cees. *Jan Tschichold; Master Typographer: His Life, Work & Legacy*. London: Thames & Hudson, 2008.

De Jong, Cees; Purvis, Alston. *Type: A Visual History of Typefaces and Graphic Styles 1628-1900*. Berlin: Taschen, 2013.

Eason, Ron and Rookledge, Sarah. *Rookledge's International Directory of Type Designers*. New York: The Sarabande Press, 1994.

Elam, Kimberly. *Typographic Systems*. New York: Princeton Architectural Press, 2007.

Eskilson, Stephen J. *Graphic Design: A New History*. New Haven: Yale University Press, 2007.

Evans, Poppy and Thomas, Mark A. *Exploring the Elements of Design*. New York: Thomas Delmar, 2008.

Fredl, Friedrich; Ott, Nicolaus; Stein, Bernard. *Typography: An Encyclopaedic Survey of Type Design and Techniques Throughout History*. New York: Black Dog & Leventhal Publishers, 1998.

Frutiger, Adrian. *Typefaces—The Complete Works*. Berlin: Birkhauser, 2009.

Gill, Eric. *An Essay on Typography*. New York: Penguin Group (USA) Inc., 2013.

Goudy, Frederic W. *Typologia*. Berkeley, University of California Press, 1977.

Haley, Allan; Poulin, Richard; Tselentis, Jason; Sedden, Tony; Leonidas, Gerry; Saltz, Ina; Henderson, Katryn, with Alterman, Tyler. *Typography Referenced*. Beverly: Rockport Publishers, 2012.

Heller, Steven and Fili, Louise. *Stylepedia*. San Francisco: Chronicle Books, 2006.

Hill, Will. *The Complete Typographer: A Manual for Designing with Type*. Upper Saddle River: Pearson Prentice Hall, 2005.

Kane, John. *A Type Primer*. London: Laurence King, 2002.

Kinross, Robin. *Modern Typography: An Essay in Critical History*. London: Hyphen Press, 2004.

Leborg, Christian. *Visual Grammar*. New York: Princeton Architectural Press, 2004.

Lupton, Ellen. *Thinking with Type: A Critical Guide for Designers, Writers, Editors, and Students*. New York: Princeton Architectural Press, 2004.

McLean, Ruari. *Jan Tschichold: A Life in Typography*. New York: Princeton Architectural Press, 1997.

Meggs, Philip B.; Purvis, Alston. *A History of Graphic Design*. Hoboken: John Wiley & Sons, 2006.

Müller, Lars. *Helvetica: Homage to a Typeface*. Zurich: Lars Müller Publishers, 2013.

Osterer, Heidrun. *Adrian Frutiger Typefaces: The Complete Works*. Switzerland: Birkhäuser Architecture, 2008.

Pevsner, Nikolaus. *Pioneers of Modern Design: From William Morris to Walter Gropius*. New Haven: Yale University Press, 2005.

Pohlen, Joep. *Letter Fountain [on printing types]*. Cologne: Taschen, 2011.

Poulin, Richard. *The Language of Graphic Design: An Illustrated Handbook for Understanding Fundamental Design Principles*. Beverly: Rockport Publishers, 2011.

Re, Margaret. *Typographically Speaking: The Art of Matthew Carter*. New York: Princeton Architectural Press, 2003.

Rosendorf, Theo. *The Typographic Desk Reference, Second Edition*. Oak New Castle: Knoll Press, 2016.

Ruder, Emil. *Typography*. New York: Hastings House, 1971.

Samara, Timothy. *Design Evolution: Theory into Practice. A Handbook of Basic Design Principles Applied in Contemporary Design*. Beverly: Rockport Publishers, 2008.

Samara, Timothy. *Typography Workbook*. Beverly: Rockport Publishers, 2004.

Shaw, Paul. *Helvetica and the New York City Subway System*. Cambridge: MIT Press, 2009.

Shaw, Paul. *The Eternal Letter: Two Millennia of the Classic Roman Capital*. Cambridge: MIT Press, 2015.

Smeijers, Fred. *Counterpunch: Making Type in the 16th Century, Designing Typefaces Now*. London: Hyphen Press, 1997.

Spencer, Herbert. *Pioneers of Modern Typography*. Cambridge: MIT Press, 1983.

Spiekermann, Erik. *Hello, I am Erik: Erik Spiekermann: Typographer*. Designer, Entrepreneur. Berlin: Gestalten, 2014.

Spiekermann, Erik and Giner, E. M. *Stop Stealing Sheep and Find Out How Type Works*. Mountain View: Adobe Press, 1993.

Strizver, Ilene. *Type Rules! The Designer's Guide to Professional Typography*. Hoboken: John Wiley & Sons, 2014.

Tschichold, Jan. *The New Typography*. Berkeley: University of California Press, 2006.

VanderLans, Rudy; Licko, Zuzana. *Émigré: Graphic Design into the Digital Realm*. London: Booth-Clibborn Editions, 1993.

White, Alex. *The Elements of Graphic Design: Space, Unity, Page Architecture, and Type*. New York: Allworth Press, 2002.

Wozencroft, Jon. *The Graphic Language of Neville Brody*. New York: Rizzoli International Publications, 1994.

Index

Index continued

P – Z

Credits

About the Author

As Co-founder, Design Director, and Principal of Poulin + Morris Inc., Richard Poulin has directed visual communications programs for clients including Brooklyn Botanic Garden, Brooklyn Museum, Carnegie Hall, William J. Clinton Presidential Foundation, Cornell University, Lycée Français de New York, Mandarin Oriental Hotel Group, Morgan Stanley, New York Historical Society, New York Law School, The New York Public Library, Novo Nordisk, NPR, The Norman Rockwell Museum, School of American Ballet, Smithsonian Institution, Syracuse University, Vassar College, W Hotels and Resorts, and Yale University.

His work has been published in periodicals and books worldwide, is in the permanent collection of the Library of Congress, and has received awards from American Institute of Architects (AIA); The American Institute of Graphic Arts (AIGA); *Applied Arts*; Art Directors Clubs of New York, Los Angeles, and San Francisco; *Communication Arts*; *Creative Quarterly*; *Graphis*; *ID*; *Print*; Society for Experiential Graphic Design (SEGD); Society of Publication Designers; and Type Directors Club.

Richard is a Fellow of the Society for Experiential Graphic Design, the organization's highest honor, and a recipient of a research grant from the Graham Foundation for Advanced Studies in the Fine Arts. He is also the author of several award-winning books including *The Language of Graphic Design: An Illustrated Handbook for Understanding Fundamental Design Principles*; *Typography Referenced* (coauthor); and *Graphic Design + Architecture: A 20th-Century History*, all published by Rockport Publishers; and *Archigraphia Redux*, published by Graphis.

Since 1992, he has been an adjunct professor at the School of Visual Arts in New York City and was formerly an adjunct professor at The Cooper Union. Richard is a frequent lecturer and visiting professor at universities and educational institutions including Carnegie-Mellon University, The Maryland Institute College of Art, Massachusetts College of Art, North Carolina State University, Syracuse University, University of the Arts, University of Cincinnati, and University of Washington.

Acknowledgements

This book is dedicated to Doug Morris, my husband and partner in life, work, and love, who has always given me the time, freedom, and support to pursue my dreams.

Design School: Type would not have been possible without the assistance and generous contributions of so many people. My sincere appreciation to all of the graphic designers, educators, students, and colleagues for generously contributing examples of their work.

A special thanks to Rockport Publishers for their continued support.

And, to James Evans, my editor and associate publisher at Quid Publishing (London) for his invaluable guidance and insights.

To Erik Herter and Derek Koch, my colleagues at Poulin + Morris Inc., who helped design this volume with a level of detail and nuance that I did not fully appreciate when we started this project. Their invaluable insights, contributions, and creativity in the organization and design of this volume are deeply appreciated.

And as always, to my students—past, present, and future, who continue to inspire and challenge me every day.

Colophon

Design School: Type was designed and typeset by Poulin + Morris Inc., New York, New York. Digital type composition, page layouts, and type design were originated on Apple iMac computers, utilizing Adobe InDesign CS6, Version 8.1 software.

The text of this book was set in Retina (Tobias Frere-Jones, 2016) and TheSerif (Lucas de Groot, 1994), produced by Frere-Jones Type, Brooklyn, New York and Lucas Fonts, Berlin, Germany, respectively.

Credits

Author and Design Director: Richard Poulin
Creative Director and Designer: Erik Herter
Designer: Derek Koch